Good Housekeeping
Book of Quilt Making

BY VERA P. GUILD

ACKNOWLEDGMENTS
Photographic credits: Front cover, Bill Margerin,
Will Rousseau, Justin & Barbara Kerr.
Back cover, Myron Miller.

Howard Graff, Pages 25, 28-29, 31-32, 65, 66-67, 70-71, 80.
Bill Margerin, Pages 17, 26-27, 30, 68-69, 76-77.
Will Rousseau, Pages 18-19, 20-21.
Justin & Barbara Kerr, Pages 74-75.
Myron Miller, Pages 78-79.
Otto Fenn, Pages 22-23.
Feliciano, Page 24.
Norma Nishimura, Pages 72-73.

Quilts shown on pages 17, 18, 22, 68, 74, 76, and 80
are from the Kutztown Folk Festival, Kutztown, Pennsylvania.

ISBN 0-87851-017-6

Library of Congress Catalog Number 76-4189

CONTENTS

Good Housekeeping
Book of Quilt Making

INTRODUCTION

American quilts were born of necessity. Pioneer homes were cold and drafty and frontier women made them warm with quilts and comforters on beds, with quilted curtains at windows and with quilted padding on chairs or any place where protection and warmth were needed. Even quilted petticoats were worn. These early homemakers saved and utilized every scrap of good fabric from worn garments and anything left from sewing new ones and fashioned them into quilts. The pieced or "patchwork" quilt is uniquely American.

The earliest quilts were pieced in "hit or miss," or crazy-quilt patterns and without much design. Gradually simple geometric patterns evolved in stripes and blocks. These became more and more elaborate and were given names that were significant of the place and the times, such as Log Cabin, Turkey Track, Arrowhead, Shoo Fly, Rising Sun, Melon Patch. Some had Biblical implications, such as Jacob's Ladder, Rob Peter to Pay Paul, Cross and Crown, or Hosanna, and some were politically influenced, such as Clay's Choice, Nelson's Victory, Whig Rose, or Free Trade Block. Many patterns were carried to other parts of the country and given new names.

Appliqued quilts may have evolved from patching the worn places on old quilts but the real appliqued quilt, with its base of a large piece of fabric with the design applied on top, could not come about until times were better and fabric more plentiful. These were a luxury and became show pieces to be used on special occasions or given as gifts. A young girl was expected to have a number of quilts as part of her dowry as well as the bride's own quilt, the elaborate blocks of which were made by her friends.

The quilting bee served to bring women together in groups and became a social occasion. When a quilt top was pieced and ready for the frame the neighbors were invited in to help with the quilting. After the top was pieced a backing had to be made. This often was of wide stripes (and still is), or of another simple arrangement, probably designed to fit the fabric at hand. The earliest quilts were of handwoven fabric, and few are left. They were stuffed with straw, feathers or cotton and were tied front-to-back at intervals. These were known as comforters. Rows of hand stitching (quilting), to hold the layers together, came later. Quilting patterns, at first quite simple, became more and more elaborate. Eventually some quilts were made in one solid color (often white), with intricate quilting as their only decoration.

In place of straw, feathers, and crude cotton, we now have fine cotton batting ready prepared to lay on the quilt back before the top is placed in position. We also have a wealth of fabrics in both printed and plain colors to challenge the imagination of the most avid quilt makers. Although quilts were originally made for very practical reasons, the art of quilting has never entirely died out. Periodically a new wave of enthusiasm overtakes us and quiltmaking and collecting become newly popular. We are now going through such a period.

The quilt is an American tradition and considered by some to be an art form. The old geometric patterns have great style and are especially suited to modern rooms. A quilt made from pieces left from dresses worn by family and friends is a lovely thing to own or inherit.

In this book you will find patterns and directions for making many of the old familiar designs and also some more unusual ones.

Vera P. Guild

GENERAL INSTRUCTIONS

A quilt is made up of three things: the top, which carries the design, the backing and the interlining. These three layers are sewed together by hand with fine running stitches. This is called quilting.

Choosing a pattern. The pattern you choose depends upon a number of things; (a) how skilled you are, (b) where you will be using the quilt, (c) your preference for piecing versus applique, and so on. If you are a beginner it would be well to choose a simple pattern with fairly large units. To set together tiny pieces takes patience and skill.

Size of quilt. At this point you should determine the approximate size of the quilt you wish to make. Will it be for a single, twin, double or larger bed? Most quilts today are used as spreads so your calculation must include the actual mattress size plus drape. Like any spread, a quilt can be used with a dust ruffle or drop to the floor. Some patterns

look best if all the blocks are of the pieced design; others look more attractive with a plain block or strip in between. This also affects the size and must be taken into consideration. If the quilt is set together with plain blocks use an odd number of blocks crosswise and lengthwise so that the corners will be alike. The quilt may be planned with or without a border and the border may be wide or narrow. Sometimes quilts are made so the pieced blocks lie on top of the bed and the drop all around is border, which may be plain or pieced in rows. Make a rough drawing of how the quilt is to look before starting to make it.

Choosing a color. Colors are important but also a personal matter. If you want your quilt to blend with a certain color scheme, this gives you a starting point. If you want to reproduce or approximate an old time color arrangement you should study many old quilts.

Choosing a fabric. For the quilt top choose fabrics with a firm but soft texture such as fine percale, lightweight fine muslin or broadcloth. Use a thin interlining, (cotton batting), since it allows for finer stitches and closer rows of quilting.

If your pattern directions do not specify the amount of fabric needed you will have to figure it yourself. Draw an actual size block and figure from there. Multiply this amount by the number of blocks you need and add what you need for borders.

One of the most important things to keep in mind is to use the best materials you can afford. It is the height of foolishness to put all the work involved in making a quilt into cheap fabric that will not wear and may fade in washing.

Making a pattern and cutting the pieces. After choosing the design enlarge it as directed. (See "How to Enlarge a Pattern," page 15.) Then place tracing paper over the design and trace each unit separately and exactly. Determine how many of each unit is required for a block and then for the entire quilt. Allow one fourth inch all around each unit for seams. With the paper pattern as a guide, cut a permanent pattern of each unit from medium weight cardboard, (or use fine sandpaper because it does not slip on the fabric). Lay the pattern for each unit on the fabric with

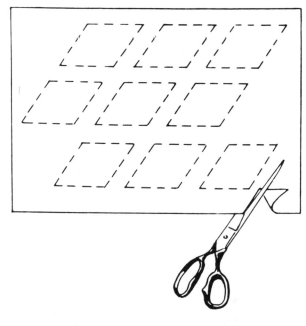

straight edges following the grain of the fabric. Cut accurately. Separate colors and units and run a thread through each pile.

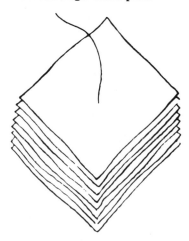

If you are following specific instructions for making a certain quilt, (such as those in this book), study them carefully before you begin.

Piecing. A rule of patchwork is to join the pieces or units from the center out. Lay two pieces with right sides together and join them on the seam line with fine running stitches. Keep in mind that exactly ¼" has been al-

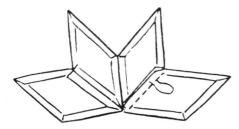

lowed for seams. Start and stop exactly on the seam line at corners, so seam allowance will be free when you join the next piece. Use a short length of thread and be careful not to stretch any bias edges. Give special attention to corners where more than two pieces meet, so that a perfect joining is made. Press seams open as you go, it makes a better looking quilt.

Setting the quilt together. There are many ways of varying the "set"; first work out on paper the one you will use. After the blocks are finished, join blocks in strips and sew the strips together. Put the border on last. Pieced blocks are often alternated with plain blocks

or plain strips are set between them in both directions. Make all seams match and press the whole top carefully after it has been set together.

Preparing the backing. The backing is made of widths of fabric stitched together. Usually a 36" width is used in the center and a narrower strip on each side. Remove selvages before sewing strips together. The backing is usually cut a little larger than a pieced top, because the latter has more "give." If you wish to bring the edge of the backing over the top for a binding, as is often done, cut the backing about three inches larger all around.

Marking the quilting pattern. The quilting pattern may be marked on the quilt before or after putting the quilt into the frame. Simple patterns, such as evenly spaced diagonal lines, can be drawn directly on the quilt with pencil and ruler. For curves and circles use a cup or plate for a guide. Mark lightly with pencil.

A plain all-over pattern, such as diagonal lines or diamonds, is very effective. Change the direction of the lines for variation. A quilt with plain and pieced blocks is more effective if the plain blocks are quilted more elaborately than the pieced ones. Sometimes the design of the pieced or applique block is used for a quilting pattern on the plain blocks and the background is filled with diagonal lines. If the marking is done in the frame, mark all reachable space, then quilt and roll; repeat until quilting is finished.

Interlining. Cotton batting is most often used and is most practical. One batt is usually sufficient for a single-size quilt. They are sold in different sizes.

Putting layers together. Lay the quilt backing flat on the floor, wrong side up, and smooth it out. Place cotton batting on top, one strip next to another (do not overlap). Arrange batting in an even thickness and with no wrinkles. Lay the quilt top in place, right side up, and pin and baste all three layers together (See Diagram).

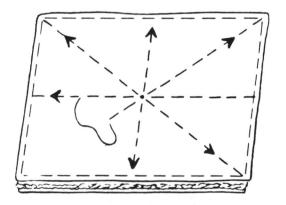

Quilting frames. Good quilting results require the use of a frame to hold the work taut while it is being quilted. A quilting frame may be made of four strips of wood, two short bars

and two long bars, and a clamp at each corner for control. The corners must be kept at right angles. Tack a tape or strip of muslin along the length of each bar, and sew the top and bottom edges of the quilt to the tape. Roll the quilt on one long bar until it is the length of the short bars. The exposed part of the

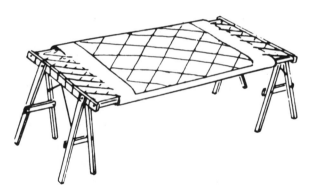

quilt should be as much as can be reached comfortably from either side. Clamp the frame corners. To hold quilt sides taut, sew over and over with heavy thread through the edges of the quilt and around the short bars. A large hoop, 22" or more in diameter, can be used instead of a frame. Begin in the center of the quilt and work outward.

Quilting. Use a short needle especially made for quilting to speed the work. Also use quilting thread, which is strong, smooth and less likely to knot. Use a short length of thread, and pull the knot through to the batting so it will not show. Place the forefinger of your left hand over the spot where the needle should come through. With your right hand, push the needle through the quilt from below until it touches the finger. Pull thread through with the right hand; the left forefinger is now put under the quilt. With your right hand push needle down through quilt to touch forefinger. Pull thread through with right hand. Continue working in this fashion. This upward and downward movement through the layers is the only correct way to quilt, according to many old time quilters. However, with experience, several small stitches can be picked up at one time as in regular hand sewing. Fasten the end of each thread securely by running it between the layers. When you are working in a frame and have quilted all the area within reach, undo the threads at the sides, roll the quilt until a new area is exposed and continue. After quilting has been completed, use art gum to erase any pencil lines. Then bind the edges of the quilt.

Applique. Quilts made in applique require an entirely different technique from that for making pieced quilts. To applique, one piece is laid on another and its edges are turned under and secured with fine hemming stitches.

Applique patterns are often designed for blocks. In these cases the general rules for planning the quilt and setting it together are the same as for a pieced block design. However, many applique quilt patterns have large center designs with borders or other all-over type designs. For these designs the top of the quilt must be in one piece. Usually they have a wide panel down the center and a narrow panel on each side. These panels are sewn together before the applique design is begun.

How to applique. If you are not using a ready-stamped quilt pattern, trace the design parts and make a cutting pattern of each piece with heavy paper or thin cardboard. Lay the cutting pattern on the fabric and trace around it. Cut out, allowing ¼" for turning under.

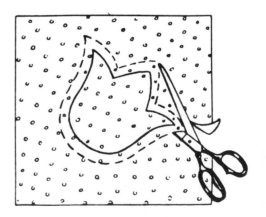

The traced line is the turn-under line. Place the patch where it belongs, match and pin carefully, turn under on the line and baste in place. Clip corners and curves where necessary. Let flowers, buds and leaves overlap stems. Turn under all raw edges unless they end at the edge of a block and will be sewn in with the seam. Using No. 70 thread sew on patches with invisible hemming stitches, barely catching the edge of the patch and keeping its true shape.

Caring for quilts. A beautiful quilt deserves the best of care and a well-made one should keep its proper shape after many launderings. Do not let a quilt become too soiled. You may wash it in an automatic washer using the short washing cycle intended for fine fabrics and a mild soap or detergent. Never wring a quilt by hand or spin dry in the washer. Instead arrange the wet quilt on a clothesline, matching corners, and let it drip dry. Do not iron. After washing, examine it carefully to see if any quilting stitches have broken; if so, repair them at once. Fine quilts may be dry-cleaned.

TO ENLARGE A DESIGN OR PATTERN

Almost any design can be enlarged by following these simple instructions.

A quick method is to have a full-size photostat of the chart made according to the scale under the chart. (Check your classified directory for a photostat service.)

Or you can enlarge it yourself as follows: Use a piece of plain paper (wrapping paper will do), large enough to accommodate the design. Start with a perfect right angle at one corner and mark the paper in the same number of squares as indicated on the chart; each square will be ½", 1", or 2", etc., according to scale at bottom of chart. Draw the design in each square. Cut out the paper pattern, then cut the fabric. Trace any inner markings onto fabric according to pattern and instructions.

If you wish to enlarge a design which is not already squared off you can do this yourself. First determine the finished size you want in inches in both directions. Draw this "grid", (squares), over the design using the same number of squares but smaller. Then proceed as above.

CROSS AND CROWN QUILT

Finished Size 94" x 94"

When carried out in two colors as shown, the Cross and Crown Quilt makes a striking focal point in a room.

Photograph shows quilt (about 94" square) containing 25 pieced blocks joined together with pieced strips, 2" inner border, 7" outer border and 3/8" binding.

MATERIALS:

5½ yards 36" wide fine percale or broadcloth, blue

14½ yards wide, fine percale or broadcloth, white

8¼ yards of this white is for backing

Thin cotton or synthetic batting

White quilting thread

Short needle

Quilting frame or hoop

Directions for quilt start on page 33.

17

MISSOURI STAR QUILT

Finished Size 92" x 108"

Shown here is a beautiful interpretation of the old Missouri Star Quilt pieced in printed and plain fabrics.

Directions for quilt start on page 37.

TRIPLE IRISH CHAIN QUILT

Finished Size 84" x 84"

Quilts are being used in many ways other than bed coverings. This Triple Irish Chain Quilt makes an eye catching table cover.

Directions for quilt start on page 41.

LOG CABIN QUILT

Finished Size 94" x 96"

The Log Cabin Quilt is a time-honored traditional pattern which can be interpreted in many ways depending upon how the light and dark colors are placed.

Here also is a variety of pillows including Log Cabin, Biscuit (lower center), Rosette (upper center) and the Diagonal pillow.

MATERIALS:

6 yards 36" wide green print cotton fabric

About 1 yard each (36" wide) brick red, blue, yellow and pink print cotton

8¼ yards 36" wide fabric for backing

Cotton or polyester batting

Sewing thread

Quilting thread

Directions for quilt start on page 44.
Directions for pillows start on page 51.

FRIENDSHIP KNOT QUILT

Finished Size 92" x 107"

The Friendship Knot Quilt, sometimes known as the Starry Crown, is a lovely, bold pattern. Calico prints plus plain bring out the distinctive design. The quilt is made with 30 pieced blocks joined together, with a 9" border and ½" binding.

MATERIALS:

9 yards 44" wide yellow fine
   percale or broadcloth
36" wide fine calico prints —
   4½ yards red, 2 ½ yards black
9¾ yards 36"-44" wide light
   orange percale for backing
Thin cotton or synthetic quilt
   batting to cover an area
   98" by 114", pieced without
   overlapping
White sewing thread
White quilting thread
Quilting frame or hoop (22" or
   more in diameter)

Directions for quilt start on page 56.

22

QUILTED PATCHWORK PILLOWS

Old quilt block designs can be made into attractive pillows. Here we have, from left to right, Nine Patch, Five Stripe and Toad in a Puddle.

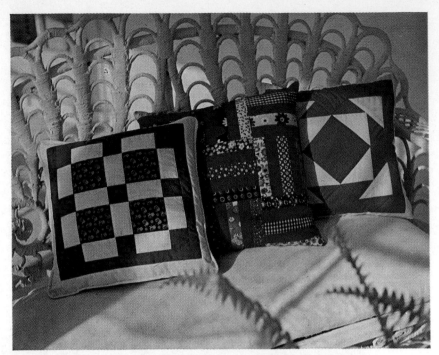

PATCHWORK SCHOOLHOUSE PILLOWS

The Old School House motif done in patchwork is shown in two versions. Any or all of these pillow designs can be repeated and set together to make a quilt.

Directions for quilted patchwork pillows start on page 59.
Directions for Patchwork Schoolhouse pillows start on page 61.

GRANNY COMFORTER

Finished Size 70" x 80"
without appendages.

The Granny Comforter is made of big squares of printed fabric sewed together and stuffed. The back is made in one piece. It is then tied at the intersections like an old fashioned comforter. Granny's head, arms and legs are made and stuffed separately and then sewed on. Fun for little girls.

Directions for quilt start on page 63.

ALPHABET COMFORTER

Finished Size 72" x 114"

Rows of cushiony blocks make up this charming child's Alphabet Quilt. A puffy border finishes it off.

MATERIALS:

3½ yards 36" wide plain cotton fabric for blocks (we used 1 yard remnants)

7 yards 36" white cotton muslin

2 yards plain, 2 yards printed 36" wide cotton fabric for letters

8½ yards 45" plain fabric for border and backing

Eight 1 lb. bags polyester batting (washable, non-allergenic, not glazed)

6 large (275 yard) spools mercerized cotton sewing thread to match border fabric

Use of zigzag sewing machine optional.

Directions for comforter and pillows start on page 82.

GOOSE TRACKS QUILT

Finished Size 66" x 77"

Goose Tracks is a lovely old pattern and suitable for any bedroom. It is usually made as shown in two colors only.

MATERIALS:
Approximately 3½ yards each of
   36" wide white cotton fabric
   and pink print fabric
4½ yards white cotton fabric
   for backing and 1 yard pink
   fabric for binding
Polyester batting for stuffing
Sewing thread

Directions for quilt start on page 85.

BASKET QUILT

Finished Size 82" x 93"

The Basket Quilt is pieced, but with appliqued handles. It is particularly suitable for a child's room. It is made with 42 pieced blocks joined together; a 2¼" inner border and 7¼" outer border.

MATERIALS:
36" wide fine calico prints —
5¾ yards blue print for outer
  border and background sections
  of basket motifs
3½ yards red print for inner
  border (surplus may be used
  as part of basket motifs)
8¼ yards dark red print for
  backing
Scraps in a variety of colors
  for basket motifs
Thin cotton or synthetic quilt
  batting for interlining
  (available in a variety of
  sizes) to cover an area
  86½" by 97¾" pieced without overlapping
White sewing thread
White quilting thread
Short needle
Quilting frame or hoop

EIGHT POINTED STAR CRIB QUILT

Finished Size 27¼" x 32"

The Eight Pointed Star Quilt design makes a charming crib Quilt.

MATERIALS:
1 yard 36" wide white percale
¾ yard 36" wide blue percale
Small amounts of print and
  solid percale
Backing and padding (see
  General Instructions)
Matching threads

Directions for Basket Quilt start on page 88.
Directions for Crib Quilt start on page 92.

VARIABLE STAR QUILT

Finished Size 69"x 90"

The Variable Star Quilt is a simple design and would be suitable for beginners. Many other color combinations are possible.

Directions for quilt start on page 94.

CROSS AND CROWN QUILT

(continued from page 17)

DIRECTIONS: To make patterns for pieced blocks (see Diagram A), trace actual size patterns given for units A, B and C. Draw a 2¼" square for unit D and a 2¼" by 5½" rectangle for unit E. Add ¼" seam allowance on all edges of each unit. Using paper as a guide, cut permanent patterns from medium-weight cardboard. Mark arrows ⟷ shown on units A, B and C to indicate straight grain of fabric. For one pieced block, cut as follows:

No. of Units	Pattern	Color
4	A	White
8	B	White
16	C	Blue
5	D	White
4	E	Blue

Cut enough for 25 pieced blocks. Group together pieces of a kind. For joining strips, cut 40 pieces 3" by 13¾" from white fabric and sixteen 3" squares from blue fabric.

Inner border — Cut four strips 2½" by 76¾" from blue fabric and four 2½" squares from white fabric.

Outer border — Cut two strips 7¼" by 80¾" (for sides) and two strips 7¼" by 94¾" (for top and bottom).

Binding — Cut 1½" wide white strips (on straight grain) to fit around entire quilt, piecing where necessary.

Assembly — Join units of pieced blocks according to Diagram A; assemble corner units first — arrows ⟷ on lower right block indicate straight grain of fabric for proper joining.

Then join units together, working from the center out. With right sides together, and using fine running stitches, take exact ¼" seams; start and stop on seam lines at corners. Be careful not to stretch bias edges. Press seams open as you go.

Next, join four horizontal joining strips to five pieced blocks to form one vertical panel (top to bottom) — see Diagrams A and B. Repeat for four more panels. For vertical joining strips, join five white strips alternately (end to end) to four blue squares. Repeat for three more vertical strips. Sew panels and strips together from top to bottom, matching seams. Run contrast basting threads centered lengthwise and crosswise on the quilt; see Diagram B.

Note: Quilt may be made wider or longer by adding joining strips at sides, top and bottom, or both.

Inner border — Join one long blue strip to each edge of assembled piece above, then white squares to corners.

Outer border — Join shorter lengths of white strips to sides of piece, then longer ones to top and bottom, including ends of side borders — see Diagram B.

Backing — Cut three 2¾ yd. lengths of fabric for backing. Join together lengthwise, taking ¼" seams. You should have a piece about 99" long and 104" wide. Measure quilt top. Backing is usually cut a little larger than pieced top.

CROSS AND CROWN QUILT

Marking quilt design — This may be done before or after putting the quilt into the frame. Simple patterns (such as the lines on pieced blocks, joining strips and inner border) can be drawn directly on the quilt with pencil and ruler — see Diagram B.

On outer border, mark center of design by running a contrast basting thread 3¼" outside seam of inner border. It is advisable to try out design on tracing paper before marking quilt. Mark one corner and about two motifs each side as indicated by curved lines on Diagram B — use ruler and cup or plate for a guide. Trace design on fabric lightly with a pencil. You are now ready to quilt.

Binding edges — Join one edge of 1½" strip of white fabric to each side edge, right sides together, piecing when necessary and taking ¼" seam. Turn in ¼" on other edge and hem over seam on backing side. Repeat for top and bottom edges, turning in ends of binding.

ACTUAL SIZE PATTERNS FOR
PIECED BLOCK DESIGN

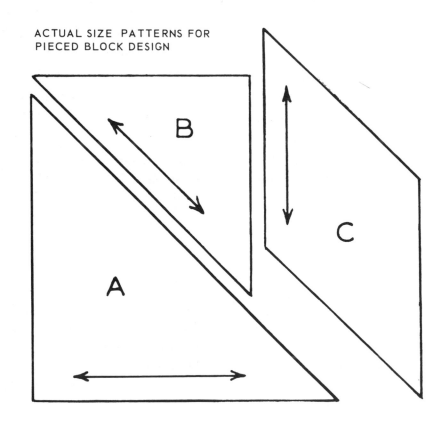

CROSS AND CROWN QUILT
DIAGRAM A

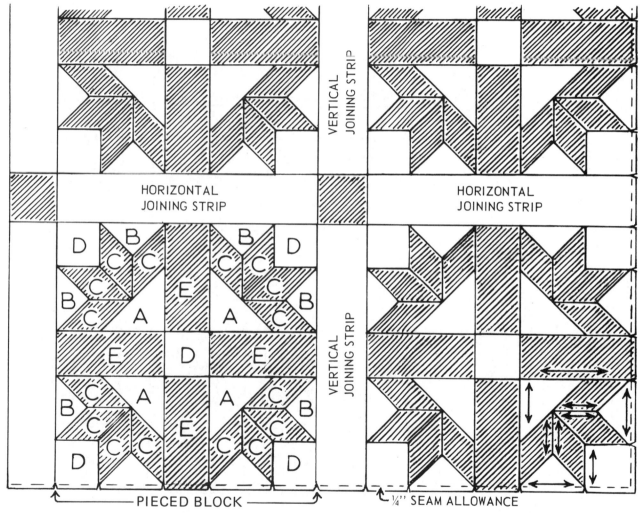

CROSS AND CROWN QUILT

DIAGRAM B

CENTER OF OUTER BORDER DESIGN (BOTTOM)

INNER BORDER

CENTER BASTINGS

INNER BORDER

CENTER OF OUTER BORDER DESIGN (SIDE)

MISSOURI STAR QUILT

(continued from page 18)

MATERIALS:

6¾ yards 36" wide calico, red
  and white print
5 yards 36" wide white fabric
  with blue dots
3¼ yards 36" wide solid red
  fabric
2½ yards 36" wide solid blue
  fabric
For padding and backing,
  see General Directions
Matching sewing threads
White quilting thread

DIRECTIONS: Patchwork center — For each pieced block, cut fabric by units A, B, C and D as indicated on patterns; place dotted arrow on straight grain of fabric when cutting unit D from white fabric with blue dots. Cut sufficient for 30 pieced blocks. Join eight units A, alternating solid red and red and white print units (see Diagram B). Next, join units B at four alternate corners. Join one blue unit C to one white with blue dot unit C at long edges. Repeat seven more times. Join blue units C together, forming four sections. Join long edges of one white with blue dot unit D to one red and white print unit D. Repeat three more times. Join each square to units C (Diagram B). Join units C to remaining inner corners of center A units. Join eight remaining units D (red and white print) to free edges of B and C, completing block. Join six pieced blocks end to end, matching seams (see Diagram C), forming panel one. Repeat four

more times. Join five panels top to bottom, matching seams.

Inner border — From solid red fabric cut lengthwise two strips 2½" by 85¾" for top and bottom and two strips 2½" x 98" for sides. Join longer strips to sides of pieced top. Join shorter strips to top and bottom, including ends of side strips (Diagram C).

Outer border — From red and white print fabric, cut on lengthwise grain two strips 5¼" by 112" for sides, and two strips 5¼" by 95¾" for top and bottom. Pin strips to corresponding edges of inner border, allowing ends to extend evenly and stitch. Pin diagonal seams at corners as shown in Diagram C. Join to seam lines at inner corners. Trim to ¼" from stitching and press open.

Backing, batting and quilting — See General Directions. Follow Diagram D for quilting, using designs given for unit B and inner border. For quilting on outer border, rule lines on true bias of fabric, spacing them 1½" apart; change direction of lines at center of sides, top and bottom, as shown in Diagram D.

Binding edges — Trim the edges on all four sides in an even line. Cut 1½" wide strips of red and white print fabric on lengthwise grain — two 95" long for top and bottom and two 112" long for sides. Join one edge of binding to top of quilt, right sides together, taking 3/8" seam. Trim away surplus at end. Turn in ¼" on other edge and hem over seam on underside. Repeat at bottom of quilt. Bind sides in same manner, turning in ends ¼".

MISSOURI STAR QUILT

QUILTING DESIGN FOR UNIT B

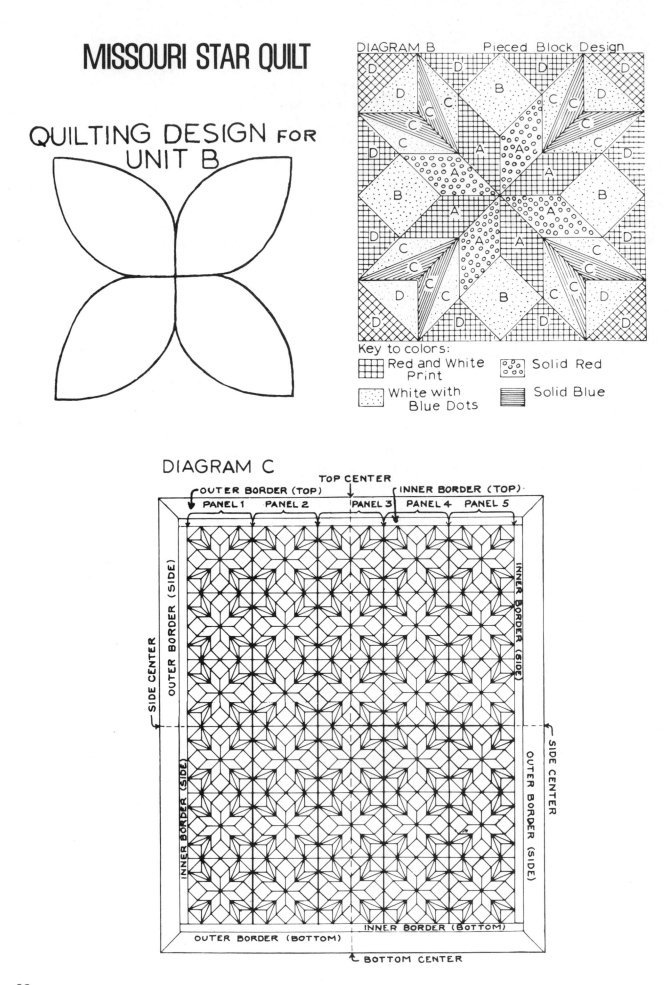

DIAGRAM B — Pieced Block Design

Key to colors:
Red and White Print
White with Blue Dots
Solid Red
Solid Blue

DIAGRAM C

TOP CENTER

OUTER BORDER (TOP)

INNER BORDER (TOP)

PANEL 1　PANEL 2　PANEL 3　PANEL 4　PANEL 5

OUTER BORDER (SIDE)

INNER BORDER (SIDE)

SIDE CENTER

INNER BORDER (SIDE)

OUTER BORDER (SIDE)

SIDE CENTER

INNER BORDER (BOTTOM)

OUTER BORDER (BOTTOM)

BOTTOM CENTER

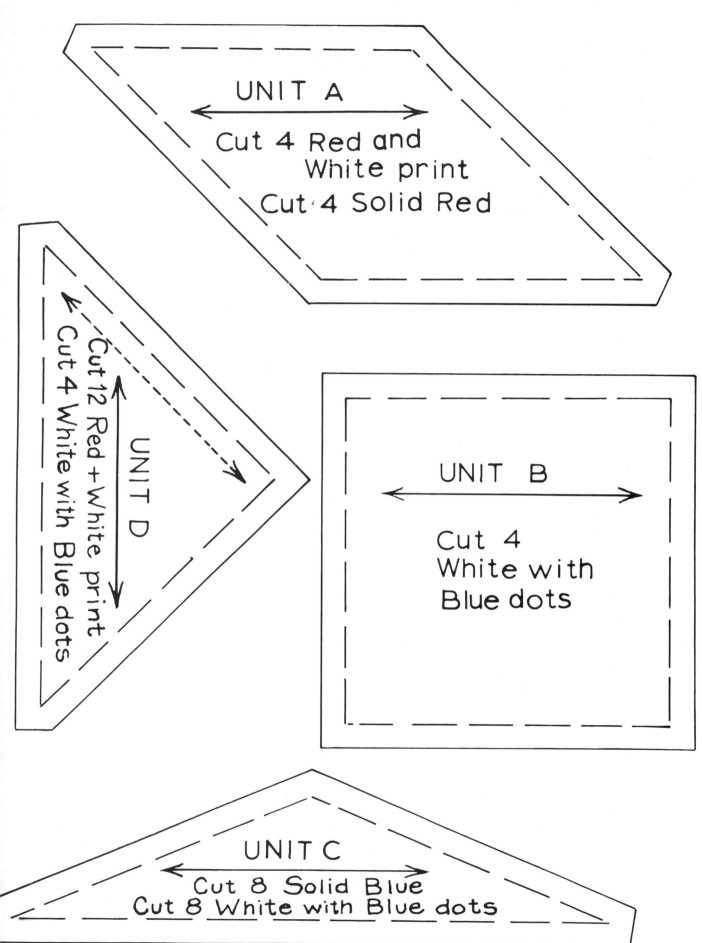

UNIT A

Cut 4 Red and
White print
Cut 4 Solid Red

Cut 12 Red + White print
Cut 4 White with Blue dots

UNIT D

UNIT B

Cut 4
White with
Blue dots

UNIT C
Cut 8 Solid Blue
Cut 8 White with Blue dots

MISSOURI STAR QUILT

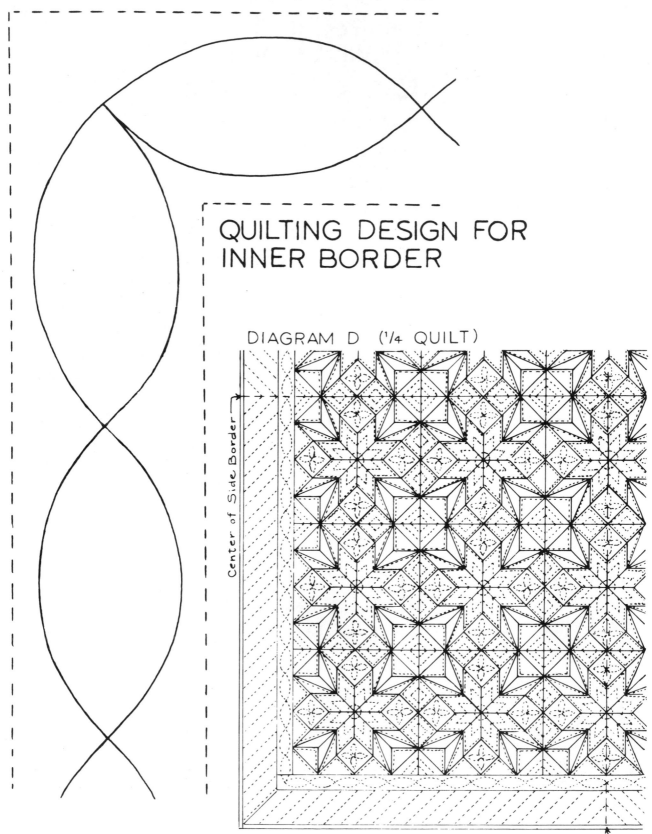

QUILTING DESIGN FOR
INNER BORDER

DIAGRAM D ('/4 QUILT)

Center of Side Border

Center of Bottom Border

TRIPLE IRISH CHAIN QUILT

(continued from page 19)

MATERIALS:

4 yards 36" wide fabric, blue
6 yards 36" wide fabric, white
For padding and backing see
General Directions
White sewing thread
White quilting thread

DIRECTIONS: Pieced block top — For each pieced block with white center and each checkerboard pieced block, cut units as indicated on patterns; make permanent patterns for units A and B as well as unit C. Cut sufficient for 25 pieced blocks with white centers and 24 checkerboard pieced blocks.

Pieced block with white center — Join two blue and white units C to form corner squares (Diagram E). Join one to each end of one unit B, then join units B and C to A.

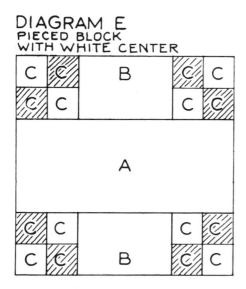

DIAGRAM E
PIECED BLOCK
WITH WHITE CENTER

Checkerboard pieced block — Join four blue and three white units C, end to end. Repeat three more times. Join four white and three blue units C, end to end. Repeat two more times. Join strips alternately lengthwise, matching seams carefully and forming checkerboard (Diagram F).

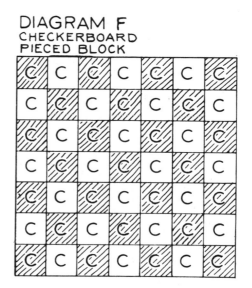

DIAGRAM F
CHECKERBOARD
PIECED BLOCK

Assembly of pieced blocks — For panel 1 (Diagram G), join four blocks with white centers alternately to three checkerboard blocks, end to end. Repeat for panels 3, 5 and 7. For panel 2, join four checkerboard blocks alternately to three blocks with white centers, end to end. Repeat for panels 4 and 6. Join the seven panels (from top to bottom), matching seams.

TRIPLE IRISH CHAIN QUILT

Inner border — From white fabric, cut on lengthwise grain, two strips 5" by 74" for top and bottom, and two strips 5" by 83" for sides. Join shorter strips to top and bottom of pieced top, ends even. Join longer strips to sides, including ends of top and bottom strips.

Outer border — From blue fabric, cut on lengthwise grain, two strips 2¾" by 83" for top and bottom, and two strips 2¾" by 87½" for sides. Join shorter strips to top and bottom, ends even. Join longer strips to sides, including ends of top and bottom strips.

Backing, batting and quilting — See General Directions. Follow Diagram H for quilting, filling in white units A and B with squares the same size as units C. Quilt inner border in same design as outer border of Missouri Star Quilt and outer border in same design as inner border of that same quilt.

Binding edges — Follow instructions given for Missouri Star Quilt, cutting four, lengthwise strips of blue fabric 1½" by 86".

For each pieced block with white center:

Unit A — Make pattern 5" by 11" (includes ¼" seam allowance)
        Cut 1 white fabric
Unit B — Make pattern 3½" by 5" (includes ¼" seam allowance)
        Cut 2 white fabric
Unit C — Pattern given
        Cut 8 blue fabric
        Cut 8 white fabric

For each checkerboard pieced block:

Unit C —   Cut 25 blue fabric
          Cut 24 white fabric

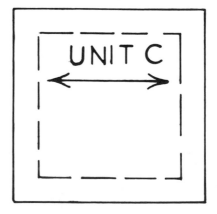

DIAGRAM G

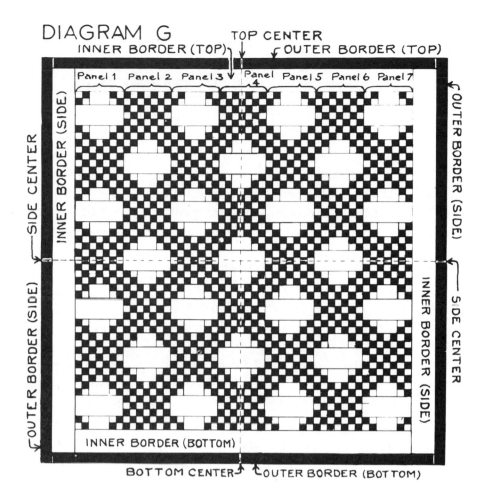

TOP CENTER

INNER BORDER (TOP) — OUTER BORDER (TOP)

OUTER BORDER (SIDE)

Panel 1 Panel 2 Panel 3 Panel 4 Panel 5 Panel 6 Panel 7

SIDE CENTER

INNER BORDER (SIDE)

OUTER BORDER (SIDE)

INNER BORDER (SIDE)

SIDE CENTER

INNER BORDER (BOTTOM)

BOTTOM CENTER — OUTER BORDER (BOTTOM)

DIAGRAM H (¼ QUILT)

Center of Side Border

Center of Bottom Border

LOG CABIN QUILT

(continued from page 21)

DIRECTIONS: (Note: ¼" seams are allowed throughout.) Study Diagram AA of the quilt top. Note that the design portion is comprised of 36 small motifs arranged in groups of four to form nine large squares. This entire center section is outlined by a narrow border made up of alternating pink and yellow triangles and this in turn is surrounded by a wide green border. Each small motif is made up of one center square and 16 strips attached one at a time in a counterclockwise direction. As these motifs are joined, they are turned in order to form the distinctive color pattern of the quilt.

Using the actual size patterns given (arrows on patterns should be placed on lengthwise grain) cut 36 pieces of each pattern number in the colors listed below.

Note: Patterns 3 and 4; 5 and 6; 7 and 8; 9 and 10; 11 and 12; 13 and 14; 15 and 16 are identical and only one pattern for each pair is given. However, cut 36 pieces for each as given below.

Pattern #1 — green
Patterns #2, 3, 10, 11 — yellow
Patterns #4, 5, 12, 13 — pink
Patterns #6, 7, 14, 15 — brick red
Patterns #8, 9, 16, 17 — blue

Assembly — After you have cut all pieces and have arranged them in separate groups for each pattern number, assemble the small motifs. Beginning with the green square and observing the ¼" seam allowance, join a yellow #2 to the square; press seams open. Following Diagram BB, continue around counterclockwise joining and pressing until square is complete. Prepare 35 remaining squares in same manner.

Making quilt top — Now join motifs in groups of four, turning squares as necessary to form color arrangement shown in Diagram AA. Finally join the nine large motifs, again turning as necessary to form the color arrangement shown in Diagram AA. For triangle border, using triangle pattern, cut 84 yellow and 80 pink triangles. Beginning and ending with yellow, make a strip of 21 yellow alternating with 20 pink triangles for each side. Join the triangle strips to each side of the center portion, then join the triangles at corners. For outer border, from green print cut two pieces 12" by 74" and two 10" by 96". Join first two pieces to top and bottom of quilt, then remaining pieces to sides. Trim away excess, if any. The quilt top is now complete.

Backing — Prepare the backing as given in General Instructions, having backing about ¼" smaller all around than quilt top so that edges of top can be brought around to back for a binding.

Assemble quilt backing, batting and top as directed in General Instructions. Baste layers together, mark quilting lines (see Diagram AA for quilting guide) and finish quilt.

DIAGRAM AA

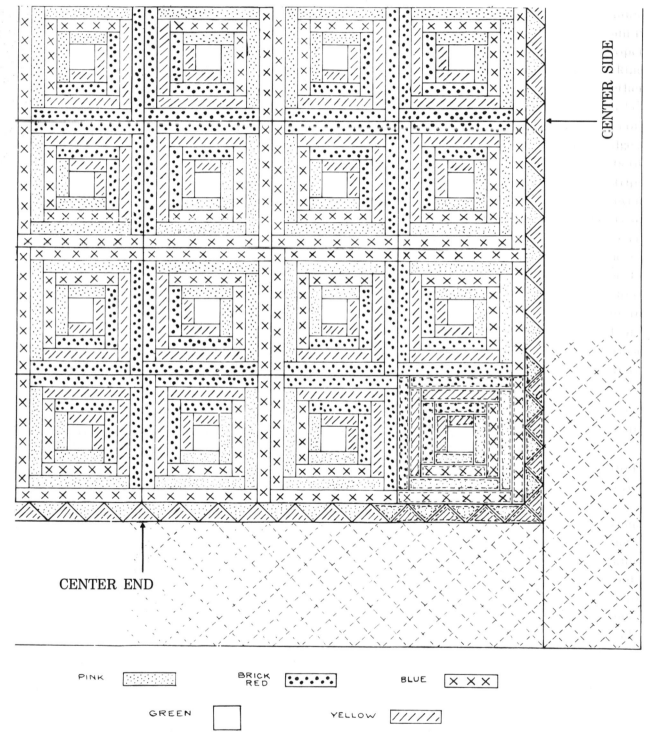

CENTER SIDE

CENTER END

PINK · · · · · · BRICK RED • • • • • • BLUE X X X

GREEN ☐ YELLOW /////

LOG CABIN QUILT

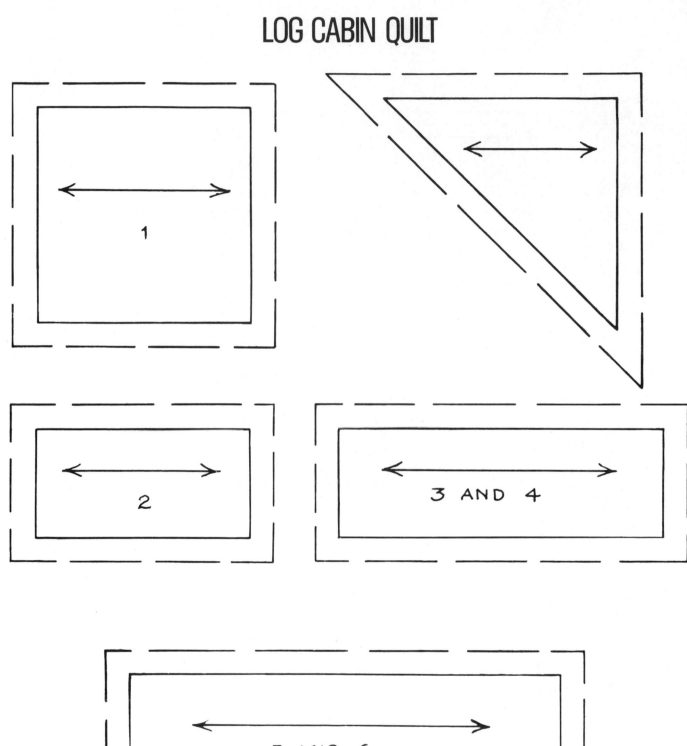

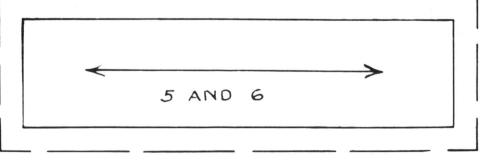

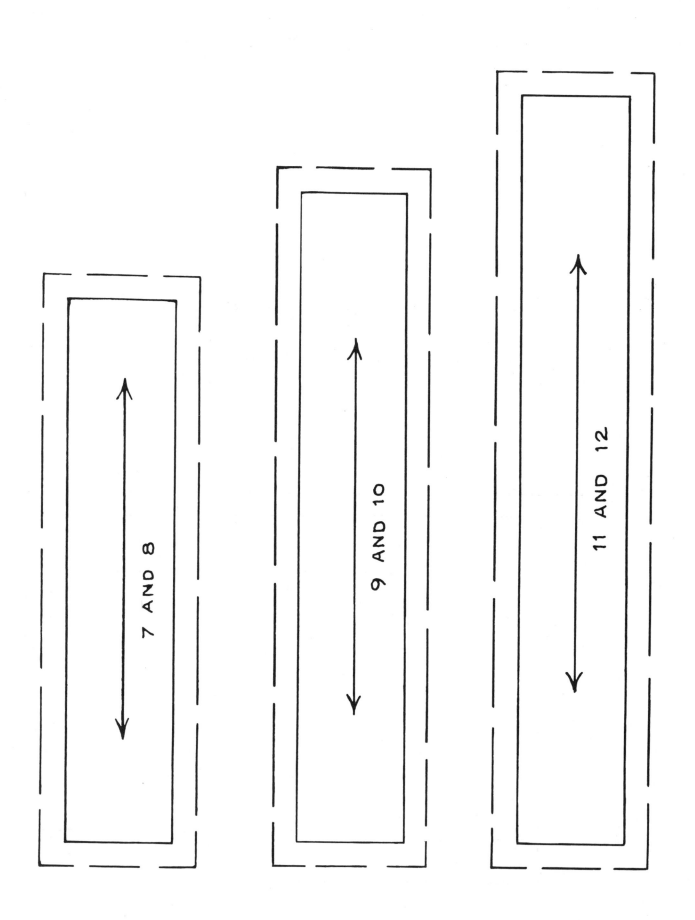

7 AND 8

9 AND 10

11 AND 12

LOG CABIN QUILT

JOIN AT ARROWS

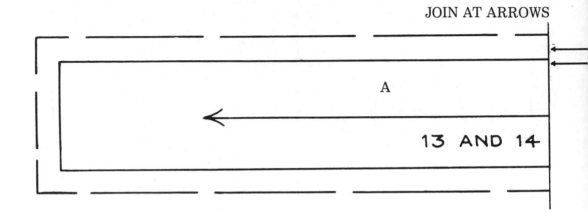

A

13 AND 14

JOIN AT ARROWS

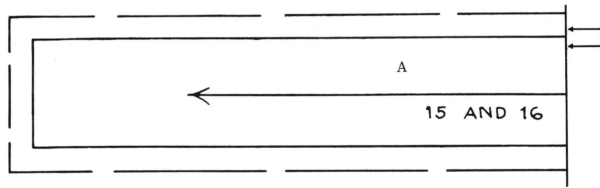

A

15 AND 16

JOIN AT ARROWS

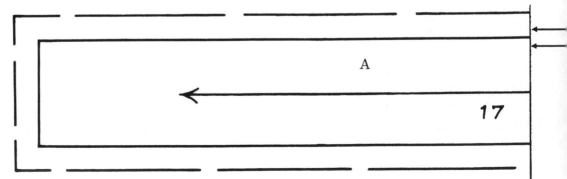

A

17

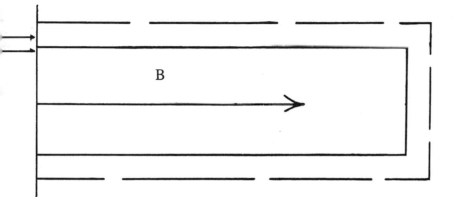

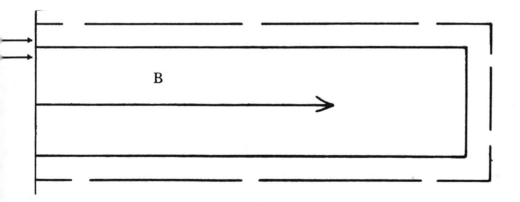

LOG CABIN QUILT

DIAGRAM BB

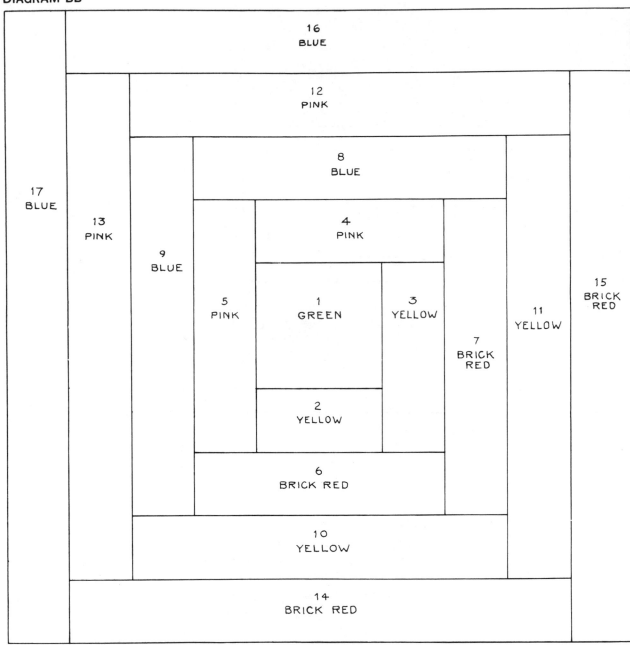

16
BLUE

12
PINK

8
BLUE

17
BLUE

13
PINK

9
BLUE

4
PINK

5
PINK

1
GREEN

3
YELLOW

7
BRICK
RED

11
YELLOW

15
BRICK
RED

2
YELLOW

6
BRICK RED

10
YELLOW

14
BRICK RED

LOG CABIN PILLOW

Finished Size 12" x 13"

(continued from page 21)

MATERIALS:

Small amounts of print and
  solid-color cotton fabrics
½ yard cotton fabric for
  pillow back
Sewing thread
14" square knife-edge
  pillow form

DIRECTIONS: Start with a 3½" square of solid-color cotton. From a print, cut a strip 3½" long and 1¾" wide. Using ¼" seam, stitch the print piece to the square (see Diagram A). Press seam open, continuing clockwise around the square. Cut another print (or solid) strip 1¾" wide and the length of the first square plus first strip width. Stitch to first piece (see Diagram B). Press seam open. Continue around, always cutting the strip 1¾" wide and the necessary length, until there are four rows of strips all around plus the center square. Press all seams open as you go. Finally, cut four strips of the same solid as the center square and add these in the same manner (see Diagram C). Place the pieced top on a flat surface with the wrong side up. With pencil or chalk, mark a 14" square, being sure to keep the solid border the same width all around. Trim excess border ¼" beyond marked line all around.

Pillow back — Using same solid as center square, cut a back for the pillow 14½" square. Right sides together, match and pin together edges of top and back. Stitch along marked line around three sides. Trim seam and corners. Turn to right side and insert pillow form. Sew open edges together by hand as inconspicuously as possible.

C

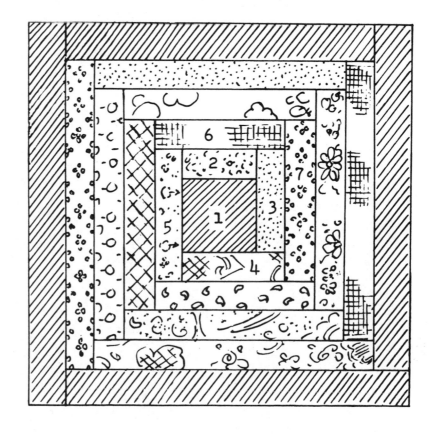

B

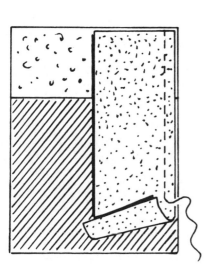

BISCUIT PILLOW

(continued from page 21)

Note: This pillow may be made any size. Ours is four squares by four squares and measures about 11½" square.

MATERIALS:
Small amounts assorted print and
   solid-color cotton fabrics
1 yard unbleached muslin
Polyester batting for stuffing
Sewing thread

DIRECTIONS: For each "biscuit", cut a 4½" square of print or solid and a 3½" square of muslin. With wrong sides together, pin the two pieces together, matching corners. Make a pleat of the excess print or solid fabric in center of three sides, pinning all pleats facing in same direction. Stitch around three sides by machine, taking ¼" seams. Now stuff the biscuit with polyester batting until quite round and firm. Close opening, forming fourth pleat, by hand. Continue in this manner to make biscuits for entire pillow. You may have biscuits front and back or just on the front.

Assembly — To assemble the pillow, thread a sturdy needle with a double strand of thread. With rounded sides facing each other pin two biscuits together along seam line. Sew together by hand, using a back stitch for strength. Sew the biscuits together in rows, then sew the rows together until you have completed the front and back. Now sew front and back together around three sides and turn to right side. Measure wrong side of pillow top and cut two pieces of muslin this size plus ¼" seam allowance all around. Stitch around three sides, trim corners and turn to right side. Fill to desired fullness with more polyester batting; close opening. Insert this form into biscuit pillow cover and close remaining open edges by hand as inconspicuously as possible.

ROSETTE PILLOW

Finished Size 14" Square

(continued from page 21)

MATERIALS:

Small amounts assorted cotton
  print fabrics
¼ yard solid-color cotton
½ yard contrasting solid-color
  cotton for pillow top and back
Sewing thread
14" knife-edge pillow form

DIRECTIONS: For each rosette, cut a 4¼"
circle of fabric. Thread needle with a double
strand of thread and, turning raw edges 1/8"
to inside, make a row of running stitch
around circle. (See Diagram D.) Draw up very
tightly to gather, tack securely and cut thread
(see Diagram E).

Make 17 solid-color rosettes and 32 assorted
print rosettes. Arrange them on a flat surface
in rows as shown in Diagram F. Carefully sew
rosettes together in rows (sew from wrong
side, taking a few tiny stitches in each rosette), then sew rows together.

From contrasting solid-color cotton, cut two
14½" squares. Stitch together around three
sides, taking ¼" seams. Trim corners, turn to
right side. Insert pillow form and close open
edges by hand. Carefully sew rosette square to
pillow top by taking tiny stitches along edges
and at corners.

D

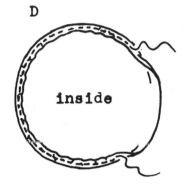

inside

E

outside

F

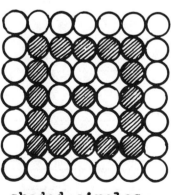

shaded circles
= solid color

DIAGONAL PATCHWORK PILLOW

Finished Size 12" x 15"

(continued from page 21)

MATERIALS:
1/8 yards each of three different
   cotton print fabrics
1 yard bias tape
3/8 yard solid-color cotton fabric
   for pillow front and back
Sewing thread
Polyester batting for stuffing

DIRECTIONS: (Note: Seam allowance is ¼" throughout.) From first print, cut a strip 2¼" by 20". Center a 20" length of bias tape on this strip; stitch along both edges of tape (see Diagram G).

From the second print, cut two strips the same size as the first strip. From the third print cut two more strips the same size. Stitch a strip cut from second print to each long edge of first strip; then stitch remaining strips to second strip in same way (see Diagram G). Press seams open.

Cut the pieced strip into sections 2½" wide (see Diagram H). Now shift the strips and stitch them together so that they form a bias effect as shown in Diagram I. Press seams open. Trim away excess to form a rectangle 5½" by 15½".

From the solid-color fabric, cut two pieces each 4" by 15½". Stitch long edges of these to long edges of patchwork piece. Press seams open. You now have the completed pillow top. Cut a back the same as top; finish and stuff as for Biscuit Pillow.

G

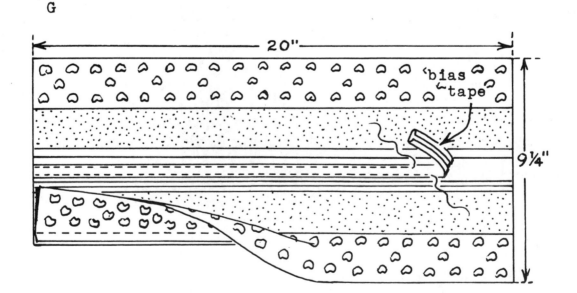

H

2½″ → ← 2½″ → ← 2½″ →

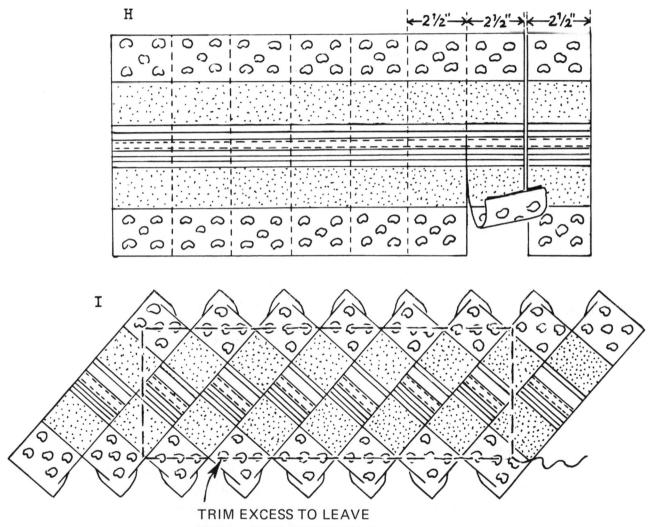

I

TRIM EXCESS TO LEAVE
5½″ by 15½″ RECTANGLE

FRIENDSHIP KNOT QUILT

(continued from page 22)

Note: Quilt may be made wider or longer by adding to width of border or by adding blocks at sides, top and bottom, or both.

DIRECTIONS: Enlarge patterns for pieced block and border quilting designs; see page 15. Trace outlines of pieced block units A, B, C, D and E (marked with arrows to indicate straight grain of fabric) onto medium-weight cardboard. Add ¼" seam allowance on all edges (squaring off ¼" from points), then cut out for use as permanent patterns.

Cutting fabric — Press fabric thoroughly. Remove all selvages. For borders: From yellow fabric, cut two strips 9¼" by 99" (top and bottom) and two strips 9¼" by 115" (sides) on lengthwise grain of fabric, without piecing. For binding: From red calico fabric, cut true bias strips 1¾" wide to total 13 yards. For pieced blocks: Trace around each cardboard for desired unit, placing arrows on straight grain of fabric. For one pieced block, cut as follows:

No. of units	Pattern	Color
1	A	Yellow
4	B	Red calico
4 right side up	C	Black calico
4 reversed	C	Black calico
4	D	Yellow
4	E	Yellow

Cut enough for 30 pieced blocks. Group together pieces of a kind.

Assembly of quilt — Join units for pieced blocks according to design chart. Join four units B together (end to end) first, then join to unit A. With right sides together and using fine running stitches, take exact ¼" seams; start and stop on seam lines at corners. Be careful not to stretch bias edges. Press seams open as you go. Join units C (and reversed C) to each unit D; join to units B. Complete short center seams in C beyond points of unit B on four sides. Join units E at corners to complete block. Join six pieced blocks (end to end) matching seams, to form one vertical panel, taking up ¼" seam allowance. Press seams open. Repeat four more times. Join five panels (top to bottom) matching seams. Press seams open.

Making border — Join 99" strips to top and bottom of assembled blocks, taking ¼" seams and extending ends evenly. Join 115" strips to sides in same manner. At corners, join ends of border strips diagonally, forming mitered seams (see Diagram A); trim away surplus fabric to ¼" from stitching and press seams open.

Marking quilting design — Run contrast basting threads, centered lengthwise and crosswise on quilt for a guide. Enlarge and trace border design onto tissue paper, then transfer to quilt, using a soft pencil. Transfer pattern to corners first, matching mitered seam lines. Continue design along border between corners, with inner points of scallops about 8" apart; space them evenly, making slight alterations to bring them closer or farther apart. The straight lines across border are 1 1/8" apart. Mark lightly with pencil (and ruler) 1½" and ½" from edges of unit A.

Backing — Cut 9¾ yard length of fabric cross-wise into three equal sections, 3¼ yards each. Remove selvages. Join together lengthwise, taking ¼" seams. The backing is usually cut a little larger than pieced top, because the latter has more "give." Press seams open.

Interlining — Place backing flat on floor, wrong side up; smooth it out. Place quilt batting on top, one strip next to another without overlapping, if piecing is necessary. Lay the quilt top in place, right side up; pin all three layers together. Starting at center of quilt,

with contrast thread, baste through all layers out to midpoint of all four edges; next, baste from center to corners. Baste outer edges together.

Binding edges — Baste all layers together ¼" inside scallop lines; cut along marked lines. Join bias strips (end to end) on straight grain of fabric; trim seams to ¼" and press open. Join one edge of binding to scalloped edges, right sides together, stretching bias at inner corners and taking 3/8" seam allowance. Turn binding over edge, turn in ¼" on free edge and hand hem over seam on underside.

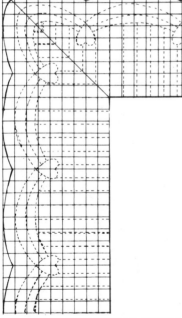

CORNER QUILTING DETAIL
SCALE: EACH SQUARE EQUALS 1"

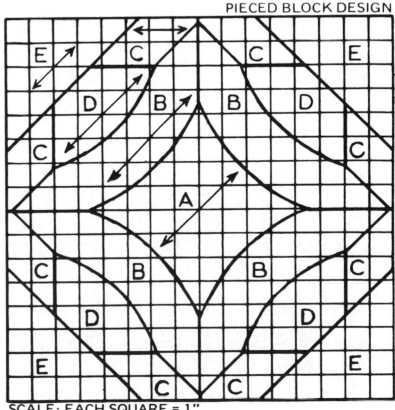

PIECED BLOCK DESIGN

SCALE: EACH SQUARE = 1"

FRIENDSHIP KNOT QUILT

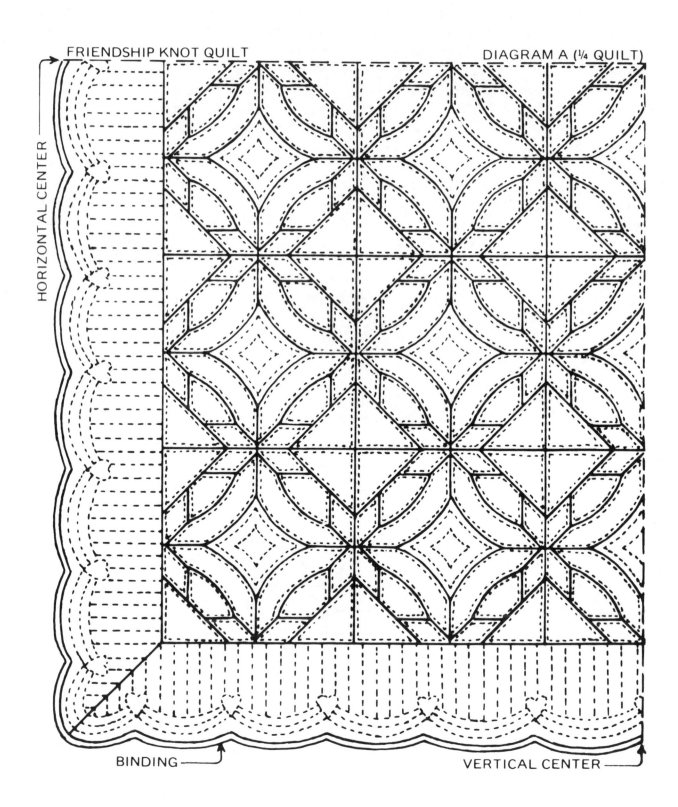

FRIENDSHIP KNOT QUILT

DIAGRAM A (¼ QUILT)

HORIZONTAL CENTER

BINDING

VERTICAL CENTER

QUILTED PATCHWORK PILLOWS

(continued from page 24)

NINE PATCH
Finished Size 14" Square

MATERIALS:

¼ yard each white and dark
  solid percale
Small amount print percale
Sewing thread
Cardboard
Fabric and zipper for pillow
  back

DIRECTIONS: Make a cardboard pattern for each unit (sizes given below include ¼" seam allowance) and cut fabric:

A — 2" square — 9 dark
B — 2" x 3¼" rectangle — 12 white
C — 3¼" square — 4 print

Border — Cut four dark strips 1½" by 12½" and four white strips 1½" by 14½". Following Diagram B, assemble and stitch pieces, excluding borders, in strips; join strips to form completed square. Press seams open. Add dark border first, then white border, trimming ends as required, press. To complete pillow, see page 60.

FIVE STRIPE
Finished Size 15" Square

MATERIALS:

¼ yard solid-color percale
Small amounts assorted con-
  trasting prints
Sewing thread
Cardboard
Fabric and zipper for pillow
  back
Polyester filler

DIRECTIONS: For pattern, cut cardboard 1½" by 5½". Placing pattern with all edges on straight grain, draw and cut 20 solid and 25 print pieces. With ¼" seams, alternating prints and solid, assemble five strips for each block; press seams open. Seven blocks have two solid and three print stripes, remaining two are the reverse — total, nine blocks. Following Diagram A, stitch blocks together in strips of three; press seams open. Stitch the strips together to form square; press. To complete pillow, see page 60.

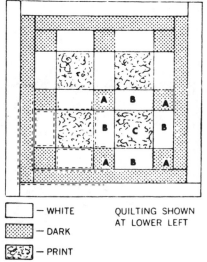

DIAGRAM B

☐ — WHITE
▨ — DARK
▧ — PRINT

QUILTING SHOWN
AT LOWER LEFT

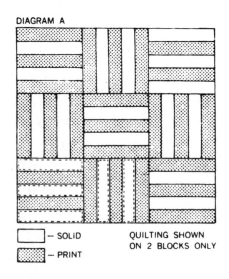

DIAGRAM A

☐ — SOLID
▨ — PRINT

QUILTING SHOWN
ON 2 BLOCKS ONLY

QUILTED PATCHWORK PILLOWS

TOAD IN A PUDDLE
Finished Size 14" Square

MATERIALS:
3/8 yard dark percale
¼ yard light percale
Sewing thread
Tracing paper
Cardboard
Fabric and zipper for pillow
  back

DIRECTIONS: To enlarge pattern from Diagram C; mark a 14" by 14" square of paper into 1" squares. Copy pattern from diagram square by square. Trace outlines of pattern units A, B, C and D. Add ¼" seam allowance on all edges of each unit and make cardboard patterns. With all right angles on straight grain, cut fabric as follows:

  A — 8 light, 4 dark
  B — 16 dark
  C — 4 dark
  D — 1 dark

For border, cut four light strips 1½" by 14½". With ¼" seams, beginning with center square, assemble and stitch pieces together as shown in Diagram C. Start and stop stitching exactly on seam line at corners, so that seam allowance is free when next piece is joined. Press seams toward edges of pillow.

Border — Follow instructions for outside border of Nine Patch Pillow on page 59.

QUILTING PILLOW TOPS:

MATERIALS:
Muslin
Thin cotton batting
Basting thread
Quilting thread

DIRECTIONS: For each pillow top, cut a square of muslin same size as patchwork piece. Cut batting same size. Patchwork piece face down, place batting on top and finally place muslin over batting. Pin. Baste by hand straight across and diagonally as in Diagram D. Working on right side, with matching thread, quilt layers together close to seams (see Diagrams A, B, and C). Remove basting. Do not press after quilting. If cording is desired, stitch to top now.

Completing Pillows — For Toad in a Puddle and Nine Patch, buy 14" pillow forms. For Five Stripe, make a form as follows: Cut two 15½" squares of muslin, stitch ¼" seams around three sides. Trim corners, turn to right side. Stuff, close opening. For pillow back, cut fabric width of top and 1½" longer. Cut in half crosswise and insert zipper. Zipper open, right sides together, pin pillow back to top; stitch around 4 sides. Trim corners, turn to right side. Insert pillow form.

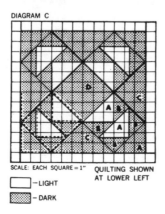

DIAGRAM C

SCALE: EACH SQUARE = 1"   QUILTING SHOWN
AT LOWER LEFT

☐ — LIGHT
▨ — DARK

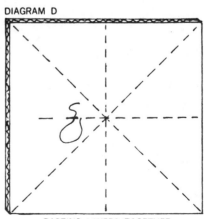

DIAGRAM D

BASTING LAYERS TOGETHER

PATCHWORK SCHOOLHOUSE PILLOWS

Finished Size 16" x 16"

(continued from page 24)

MATERIALS:

Small amounts calico print
  fabrics with dark green, red
  and orange backgrounds
Solid brown fabric
Scraps of green check, sky blue
  and bright red fabric
Matching sewing threads
½ yard each lightweight muslin
  and red firm weave cotton
Pillow form or filler

DIRECTIONS: Enlarge design. See page 15. Trace each section exactly, add ¼" seam allowance on all edges. Mark corresponding numbers on each pattern. Use to cut fabric as indicated on Key below Chart, placing edges on straight grain of fabric. For patterns #9 and #12, place right angle on straight grain; place long edges of pattern #10, short edges of pattern #11 and longest edge of #12 on straight grain. Do not remove patterns until just before joining, in order to identify pieces. Join together in numerical order, edges even; be careful not to stretch bias edges. Press seams open as you go.

Quilting top — Press entire top when completed. Cut lightweight muslin and red fabric backing the same size as patchwork top. Place a thin, even layer of fiberfill between top and muslin; pin edges together, also along seam lines to be quilted (see Chart). Stitch a scant ¼" from outer edges. Quilting may be done by hand, or use longest stitch on your machine, stitching close to seams where indicated by dotted lines on Chart.

Assembly of pillow — Join back to front, right sides together, leaving 12" opening on lower edge. Turn away corners. Turn; stuff, using ruler to pack into corners. Turn in opening edges, slip stitch closed.

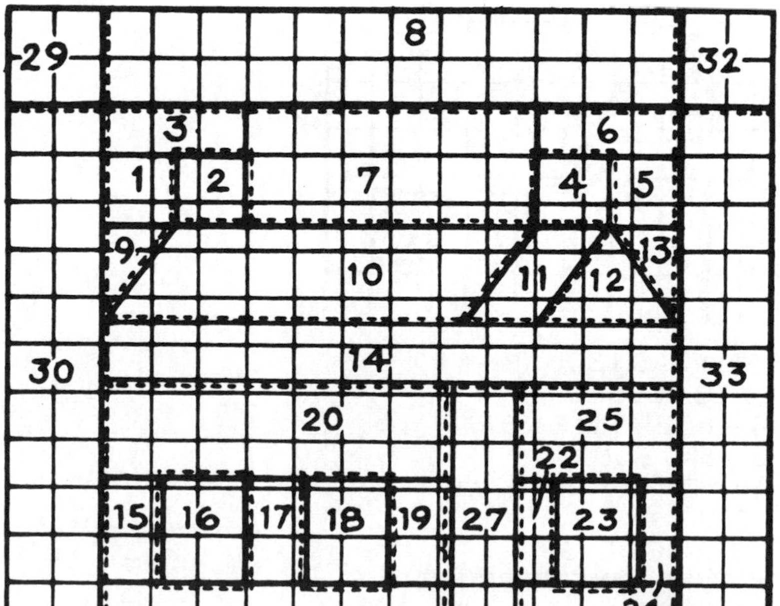

SCALE: EACH SQUARE = 1"
KEY TO COLORS:
1, 3, 5, 6, 7, 9, 13 — SKY BLUE
2, 4 — RED
8, 28, 30, 33 — DARK GREEN
  CALICO PRINT
10, 12 — GREEN CHECK
11, 14, 16, 18, 23, 27 —
  SOLID BROWN
15, 17, 19, 20, 21, 22, 24, 25,
  26 — RED CALICO PRINT
29, 31, 32, 34 — ORANGE
  CALICO PRINT

PATCHWORK SCHOOLHOUSE PILLOWS
Finished Size 8½" x 10"

MATERIALS:

Scraps of solid color and print fabrics in colors indicated on Key under Chart

Matching sewing threads

8" x 9½" pieces of lightweight muslin and red cotton

Pillow form or filler

DIRECTIONS: Enlarge design. See page 15. Trace each section exactly, adding ¼" seam allowance on all edges. Cut whole larger patterns for #2, #10 and #11, without inner cutouts. Sections #1, #6, #7 and #8 are separate pieces to be appliqued onto larger pieces. Mark numbers on each pattern. Arrows indicate straight grain of fabric on patterns #3, #4 and #5. Place all edges of remaining patterns on straight grain. Pieces are joined in numerical order, edges even; be careful not to stretch bias edges. Press seams open as you go. Turn under ¼" on two long edges and one end of section #1; slip-stitch side and upper edges to position on #2. Join sections #3, #4 and #5. Prepare and slip-stitch section #6 to #10 same as section #1. Turn under ¼" on all edges of sections #7 and #8 and slip-stitch to position on #11. Join sections #9, #10 and #11. Join two horizontal seams to complete design.

Quilting top and assembling pillow — Follow instructions for Large Pillow.

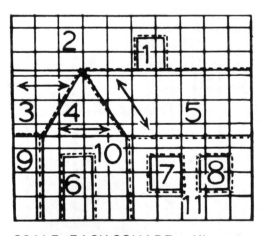

SCALE: EACH SQUARE = 1"
KEY TO COLORS
1, 6 — RED/WHITE DOTS
2, 3 — SKY BLUE
4, 10 — DARK GREEN/ WHITE DOTS
5 — STRIPED FABRIC
7, 8 — YELLOW/RED PRINT
9 — LIGHT GREEN/WHITE DOTS
11 — SOLID LIGHT GREEN

GRANNY COMFORTER

(continued from page 25)

MATERIALS:

56 squares in assorted cotton
    prints, each cut 10½ x 10½"
4¾ yards 45" wide plain or
    print fabric for backing (or
    seamless quilt back, cut 81"
    by 100", ready to use)
Dacron polyester batting 72"
    by 90" — number of rolls
    depends on thickness desired —
    we used four 1 lb. rolls
Scraps of tomato red knitting
    worsted for tufting
Yarn needle
2 yards 45" wide cotton fabric,
    pink, for head, arms and legs
1 yard 45" wide cotton fabric,
    red, for sleeves
¼ yard 45" wide cotton fabric,
    black, for shoes
3/8 yard 45" wide cotton fabric,
    brown, for hair
Matching sewing threads
Scraps of blue, red and flower
    print for 'eyes' cotton fabric for
    features plus fabric glue, or
    use iron-on fabric
Additional polyester stuffing for
    appendages
Black 6-strand embroidery cotton
½ yard elastic for sleeves

DIRECTIONS: Comforter top is planned for seven squares in width, eight squares in length. Spread all 56 squares on floor, form-ing an attractive arrangement of colors. Join eight lengthwise squares, making one long strip, taking ¼" seam allowance. Press seams open. Repeat six more times. Join lengthwise strips, matching seams carefully, taking ¼" seam allowance. Press seams open. Top should measure 70¼" by 80½".

Backing — Cut away selvages from fabric; cut two 82" lengths. Use one length center; cut other length into two 15" widths for sides. Join one to each side of center section, taking ¼" seam. Press seams open. Backing should be a little larger than top, about 72" by 82". Pin backing to top, right sides together, easing backing slightly to fit. Stitch ¼" seams along side edges and upper end, leaving bottom end open for turning. Trim seams at corners, turn and press; turn under ¼" on each opening edge, baste. Topstitch ¼" from seamed edges.

Interlining — You will need another person to help in this procedure. Lay the comforter with backing flat on floor; smooth it out. Un-roll each batting carefully; place one on top of the other, smoothing each one as you pro-ceed. Next, roll all batting together. Starting with end of roll even with opening edge of backing, unroll carefully inside comforter, one person crawling inside to unroll batting evenly, while other one holds up top. When batting has been evenly distributed, pin, then slip-stitch opening edges together. Topstitch ¼" from edge.

Tufting — While comforter is on floor, thread yarn needle with 36" length of yarn, ends

GRANNY COMFORTER

even to be used double. At intersection of each block, force needle straight down through all the layers; take a small stitch on back, forcing needle straight up. Pull yarn through, leaving 3" lengths for tying. Tie a firm double knot, then cut ends to 1" for tuft. Repeat over entire comforter, working from outer edge to the center.

Appendages (Head, Arms, Legs) — To enlarge patterns according to Chart, see page 15. Cut sections as indicated, placing center fold lines and arrows on straight grain of fabric. Seam of ¼" is allowed on all edges.

Head — Using pattern, make whole patterns for eye sections and mouth. Cut mouth from red and larger eye sections from blue fabric (or iron-on fabric); cut flower for each center of eye from print fabric. Use fabric glue to adhere other than iron-on fabrics to positions indicated on pattern. Join two head sections, right sides together, leaving neck edge open for turning. Clip seam along curves, turn. Stuff softly; turn in ¼" on opening edges, slipstitch closed.

Hair — Join top sections, right sides together, taking ¼" seams and leaving inner curved edges open 5" for turning. Trim seams at points, clip curves. Turn right side out, stuff; close openings as for head. Repeat for each side section. Pin, then hand-sew inner curved edge of top section to top seam of head; sew side sections to sides of head, lapping upper ends 2" under top section. With face section

of head against end of comforter, neck edge even with upper end and centers matching (see Diagram), machine-stitch ¼" from neck edge.

Note: If desired, snap-tape may be applied to head, arms and legs and to comforter (where they are to be joined), so they may be detached for laundering.

Arms — Join two sections for each arm, right sides together, leaving straight edge open for turning. Clip seams along curves; turn, stuff softly. Finish opening and sew to comforter, as for head.

Sleeves — Make narrow machine-stitched hem at lower edge. Cut elastic 9" long; pin to inside of sleeve along line indicated, stretching to fit flat. Stitch to position, stretching as you stitch — use zigzag stitch on machine, if available. Join sleeve seam; press open. Turn top edge ¼", draw into 2" diameter circle, fasten thread. Slip right and left sleeves over corresponding arms, pin and sew gathered edge securely at top of arms.

Legs — Pin one shoe section to lower part of each leg section, edges even. Turn in straight edge and stitch to position, baste remaining edges. Join two sections for each leg, clip seams, turn, stuff and finish openings as for arms. Using full six strands black embroidery cotton in needle, work X's on shoes and legs as indicated on pattern. Join legs to bottom of comforter same as head (see Diagram).

Directions for quilt continue on page 81.

KEEPSAKE QUILT

Finished Size 95" x 95"

This is an unusual appliqué quilt
because every block is different.
Much of the design is padded for
a raised effect.

Directions for quilt start on page 97.

PRINCESS FEATHER QUILT

Finished Size 105" x 105"

This handsome Princess Feather Quilt makes a striking bed covering. The design is over a hundred years old and is one of the loveliest of the early applique patterns.

MATERIALS:
36" wide fabric for quilt top —
9¼ yards white
2 yards red
½ yard blue or green
For padding and backing, see
General Instructions
Matching threads

Directions for quilt start on page 113.

DUTCH COUNTRY QUILT

Finished Size about 86" x 105"

Typical Pennsylvania Dutch designs such as distlefinks, (birds of good fortune), tulips and roses are applied to a modern quilt. The effect is altogether delightful. The colors may be changed to suit your decor.

Directions for quilt start on page 122.

An extra special party calls for something unusual in decoration. Why not use a quilt as a table cloth. For a large party beg or borrow a different quilt for each table. The medley quilt design is very striking used this way. For a permanent conversation piece make it in colors that suit the room in which you entertain.

MEDLEY QUILT

Finished Size 82" x 82"

This quilt, which we call the Medley, is made up of variations of familiar motifs such as the Snowflake and Rose of Sharon. Bold designs are very effective against a quiet background color.

Directions for quilt start on page 132.

"CLAY'S CHOICE" QUILT

Finished Size 76" x 90"

A simple but very effective design is this Clays Choice Quilt. It is a favorite among the pieced quilts. Make it in old-time print fabrics for authenticity. One block of the quilt makes an attractive pillow.

MATERIALS:

8½ yards 45" wide green "antique" chintz

2¼ yards 45" wide pink cotton fabric

1½ yards 45" wide rosebud print

81" by 96" sheet quilt batting

11 skeins embroidery floss

Directions for quilt start on page 138.

TURKEY TRACKS QUILT

Finished Size 82" x 97"

The Turkey Tracks design makes a simple but charming quilt. It must be carefully pieced because of the slight curve on the sides of the pieces. The border used on this quilt is particularly appropriate. The quilt is made with 50 pieced blocks and 49 plain blocks joined together with a 6" border and outer trim.

MATERIALS:

6 yards 44" wide white fine
   percale or broadcloth
36" wide fine calico prints —
2½ yards red calico print
2½ yards yellow calico print
5¾ yards 44" wide white soft
   unstarched fabric similar
   in texture to the top
   for backing
Thin cotton or synthetic quilt
   batting for interlining
   (available in a variety of
   sizes) to cover an area 84"
   by 100", pieced without
   overlapping
White sewing thread
White quilting thread (strong,
   smooth and less likely to
   knot)
Short needle
Quilting frame or hoop

Directions for quilt start on page 140.

LOG CABIN QUILT

Finished Size 86" x 106"

This is a variation of the Log Cabin Quilt design; made entirely of printed fabric with an interesting arrangement of lights and darks. It consists of 63 pieced blocks, a 2" inner border, 7½" outer border and ½" binding.

MATERIALS:

Large assortment of fine calico prints on light and dark backgrounds (for pieced blocks and outer border)

3 yards fine calico with red background (for center squares of pieced blocks, inner border and binding)

6 yards 45" wide white background small print or unstarched fabric similar in texture to the top for backing

Thin cotton or synthetic quilt batting for interlining (available in a variety of sizes) to cover an area 89" by 110", pieced without overlapping

White sewing thread

White quilting thread (strong smooth and less likely to knot)

Short needle

Quilting frame or hoop

Sew a Smashing Quilt That's Hard to Resist

Directions for quilt start on page 144.

SAMPLER QUILT

This is an antique Sampler Quilt. That is, many different old quilt block patterns have been incorporated into one quilt making it very unusual. Space does not allow instructions for all of the patterns so we have chosen several of the more familiar ones and are giving block patterns only. Follow the General Instructions for Making Quilts. By repeating one block pattern and adding borders as needed, any size can be made.

Directions for quilt start on page 146.

ORANGE PEEL QUILT

Finished Size 81" x 108"

The old Orange Peel Quilt pattern was and still is one of the favorite applique designs. Simple and effective, made here in pinks, it would be equally lovely in blues or golds.

Directions for quilt start on page 157.

GRANNY COMFORTER

(continued from page 64)

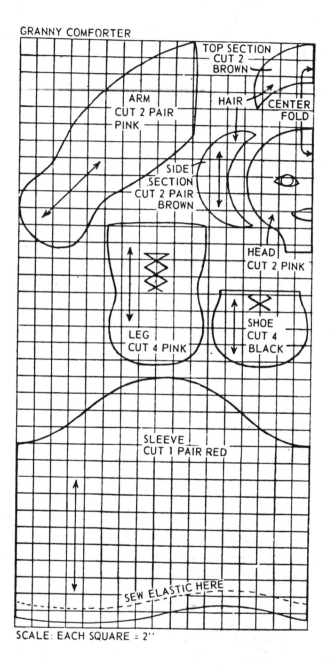

GRANNY COMFORTER

TOP SECTION
CUT 2
BROWN

ARM
CUT 2 PAIR
PINK

HAIR

CENTER
FOLD

SIDE
SECTION
CUT 2 PAIR
BROWN

HEAD
CUT 2 PINK

LEG
CUT 4 PINK

SHOE
CUT 4
BLACK

SLEEVE
CUT 1 PAIR RED

SEW ELASTIC HERE

SCALE: EACH SQUARE = 2"

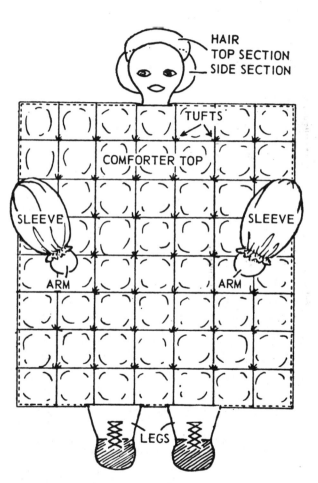

HAIR
TOP SECTION
SIDE SECTION

TUFTS

COMFORTER TOP

SLEEVE

SLEEVE

ARM

ARM

LEGS

ALPHABET COMFORTER

(continued from page 26)

DIRECTIONS: Before cutting any fabric, make certain ends are straight. To do this, clip selvage and tear across, or pull a crosswise thread and cut along the line it leaves.

Blocks — Using a sharp, soft pencil and ruler, mark fabric into 12" squares; you will need 30 squares from printed fabric, 30 from plain fabric, and 60 from white muslin.

Planning block design — Alternating plain and print blocks, spread all squares (except white muslin) on floor, forming an attractive arrangement. Number each square (within ¾" seam allowance, at one corner) according to Diagram A, in order that they may be re-arranged in same position after applique.

Letter Appliques — Enlarge patterns for letters onto heavy paper. See page 15. Next, determine which fabrics you wish to use for letters on each block (plain letters on print fabric, and prints on plain fabric); make notes. We used the entire alphabet about two-and-one-half times over. By turning every other letter upside down, the comforter has no one way direction. Pin each letter pattern onto corresponding fabric and cut out. Center each letter on corresponding block (not white muslin), baste. Use zigzag stitch on machine to applique edges; or straight stitch twice, 1/8" apart. If desired, using full six strands of embroidery cotton in needle, you may work chain stitch over straight stitching.

Assembly of blocks — Pin each block to a white muslin square; stitch ½" from edges on three sides. Stuff each softly with batting; stitch fourth side. Referring to Diagram A, pin bottom of each block to the top of block that goes below it, then stitch ¾" seam (i.e. 1 is joined to 2, then 2 to 3, 3 to 4, etc.). You should have six strips lengthwise in proper sequence, matching crosswise seams and taking up ¾" seam allowance. Press seams open.

Cutting fabric for backing and border — After straightening ends of fabric, cut two 3-yard lengths 33" wide (backing) and two 3-yard lengths 12" wide (side borders). From remaining 2½-yards fabric, cut two pieces 12" by 86" (top and bottom borders).

Backing — Pin two lengths together (right sides facing) along selvages; stitch ¾" seam, trim to ½" and press open. Lay comforter on floor, muslin side up. Place backing over comforter, right side up; pin all four sides together. Machine-stitch ¾" from all edges of comforter. Lay comforter on floor as above; pin backing to intersection of each block. Using thread doubled in needle, tack backing securely to seam allowance of blocks.

Border — Pin longer strips to each side edge of comforter, right sides together, ends even. Stitch ¾" seams (Detail a). Pin shorter strips to top and bottom edges in same manner, ends extending evenly. Stitch ¾" seams between side seams. Trim seams to ½". Make long rolls of batting and stuff border more firmly than blocks. Turn in edges ¾" and pin over seams on backing side (Detail b). Lap ends of top and bottom sections over ends of side sections, pin. Slipstitch all pinned edges to position.

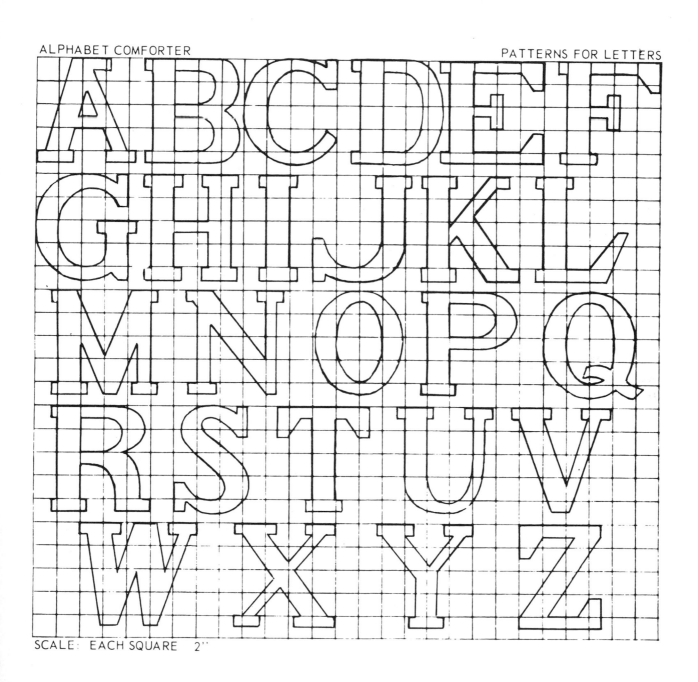

SCALE: EACH SQUARE 2"

ALPHABET COMFORTER

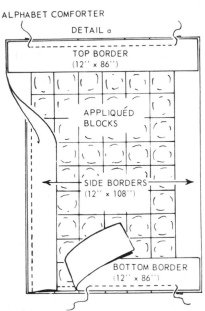

ALPHABET COMFORTER
DETAIL a

TOP BORDER
(12'' x 86'')

APPLIQUÉD
BLOCKS

SIDE BORDERS
(12'' x 108'')

BOTTOM BORDER
(12'' x 86'')

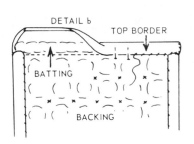

DETAIL b

TOP BORDER

BATTING

BACKING

ALPHABET COMFORTER DIAGRAM A					
1	11	21	31	41	51
2	12	22	32	42	52
3	13	23	33	43	53
4	14	24	34	44	54
5	15	25	35	45	55
6	16	26	36	46	56
7	17	27	37	47	57
8	18	28	38	48	58
9	19	29	39	49	59
10	20	30	40	50	60

ALPHABET PILLOWS

Finished Size 12" x 12"

MATERIALS:

For two pillows, use

3/8 yard each plain and
  printed 36" wide fabric
10" square of fabric for each
  letter applique
Sewing thread — same as for
  Alphabet Comforter.
Stuffing — Use Dacron polyester batting (as for Comforter),
  kapok or cut-up hylon hose

DIRECTIONS: Cut 12½" squares of fabric
for front and back of pillow. Applique letters
on front as instructed for Comforter. Join
front to back, right sides together, taking ¾"
seams and leaving one side open about 8" for
turning. Trim seams to ½", clip away corners.
Turn right side out, press. Stuff softly. Turn
in seam allowance on opening edges and slip-
stitch together.

GOOSE TRACKS QUILT

(continued from page 29)

Diagram A shows quilt containing 42 pieced blocks joined together with pieced strips, finish with ¼" binding.

DIRECTIONS: Enlarge pieced block design. See page 15. Trace one of each unit marked "A", "B", "C", "D" and "E" on tracing paper (A = 1½" square, E = 1¾" by 3¾"; make certain all edges of C are same length). Add ¼" seam allowance on all edges of each unit. Using paper as a guide, cut permanent patterns from medium weight cardboard. For pieced joining strips, cut two permanent patterns, one 1½" by 9½" and one 1½" square (¼" seam allowance is included).

Cutting fabric — Cut A, D, and E units with right angles on straight grain of fabric, B units with longest edge on straight grain, C units with one edge on straight grain. Cut joining strips and squares on straight grain. For one pieced block, cut as follows:

No. of Units	Pattern	Color
4	A	White
1	A	Pink Print
8	B	White
16	C	Pink Print
4	D	Pink Print
4	E	White

Cut enough for 42 pieced blocks. Group together pieces of a kind.

For joining strips, cut 142 long pieces and 120 squares from pink print; cut 71 long pieces and 150 squares from white fabric. For binding, cut 1-1/8" wide pink strips on straight grain fabric to fit around entire quilt, piecing where necessary.

Assembly of quilt — Join units or pieced blocks according to Design Chart; assemble corner units first — arrows ←→ on Diagram B indicate straight grain of fabric for proper joining; then join units together, working from the centers out. With right sides together and using fine running stitches, take exact ¼" seams — start and stop on seam lines at corners. Be careful not to stretch bias edges. Press seams open as you go. Join six sets of two pieces each for horizontal joining strips (Diagram B), then join long edges to seven pieced blocks to form one vertical panel (top to bottom). Repeat for five more panels (see Diagram A). Join seven sets of three pieces each for vertical joining strips, and six checkerboard squares (Diagram B), then join alternately end to end. Repeat for four more strips. Sew panels and strips together from top to bottom, matching seams. Run contrast basting threads centered lengthwise and crosswise on the quilt.

Note: Quilt may be made wider or longer by adding joining strips at sides, top and bottom or both.

Backing and interlining — For backing, stitch widths of fabric together, removing selvages before stitching. Seam fabric down center. The backing should be a little larger than pieced top. Use quilt batting (sold in a variety of sizes) for interlining. Lay the quilt backing flat on floor, wrong side up; smooth it out. Place quilt batting on top, one strip next to another without overlapping, if piecing is necessary. Lay the quilt top in place, right side up; pin all three layers together. Starting at

GOOSE TRACKS QUILT

center of quilt, baste out to midpoint of all four edges; next, baste from center to corners. Baste outer edges together.

Quilting — Use quilting frame or a large hoop (22" or more in diameter) to hold the fabric taut while it is being quilted. Begin in center of quilt and work outward. Thread short needle with short length of quilting thread, which is strong, smooth and less likely to

knot. Pull the knot through the batting so it will not show. Take small, even stitches, straight up and down through the layers; fasten end of each thread securely by running it between the layers. Quilt 1/8" each side of all seams — see Diagram C.

Finishing — Join strips for binding, end to end; press seams open. Bind top and bottom, then side edges, turning ends of binding.

DIAGRAM A

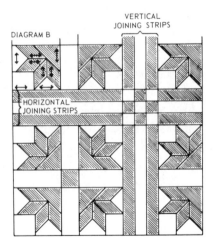

PIECED BLOCK DESIGN

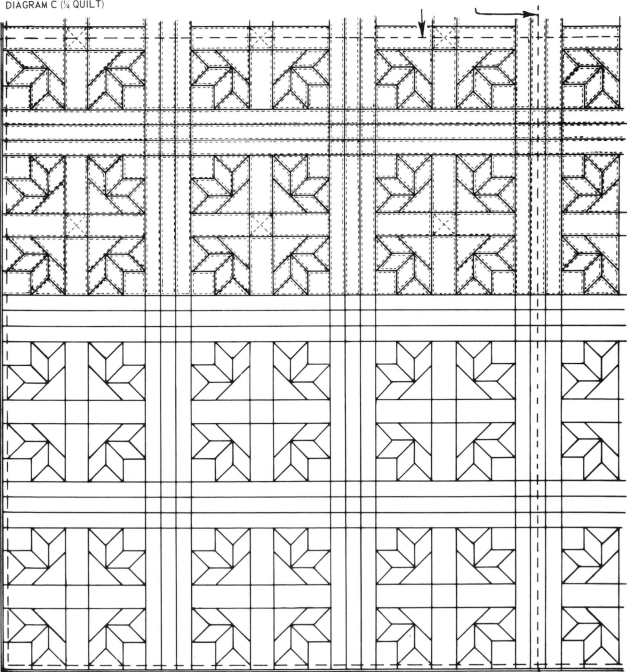

DIAGRAM C (¼ QUILT)

BASKET QUILT

(continued from page 31)

DIRECTIONS: (To enlarge pattern see page 15. Background sections A, B and C extend to lines indicated by arrows; arrow on handle F indicates straight grain of fabric.) Add ¼" seam allowance on all edges of each unit. Using paper as a guide, cut permanent patterns from medium-weight cardboard.

Cutting fabric — Remove all selvages. For outer border: from blue print, cut two strips 7¾" by 72½" (top and bottom) and two strips 7¾" by 98¼" (sides) on straight grain of fabric, without piecing. For inner border: from red print, cut two strips 2¾" by 67½" (top and bottom) and two strips 2¾" by 83¾" in same manner as above.

For pieced blocks: trace around each cardboard pattern for desired unit, placing right angles on straight grain of fabric. Arrow on unit F indicates straight grain of fabric. For one pieced block cut as follows:

No. of Units	Pattern	Color
1	A	
1	B	Blue print
2	C	
1	D	One color
5	E	scrap fabric
1	F	
11	E	Contrast scrap fabric

Cut enough for 42 pieced blocks. Group together pieces of a kind.

Assembling quilt — With right sides together and using fine running stitches, take exact ¼" seams; start and stop on seam lines at corners.

Be careful not to stretch bias edges. Join units for 21 pieced blocks (except A and F) according to Design Chart; assemble units of basket motif first. Applique basket handle to A with ends of handle even with edge of block. Then attach A to basket. Press seams open as you go. Next, join units for 21 pieced blocks with basket motif in opposite direction, large triangular unit A in upper left-hand corner instead of right-hand corner (see Diagram A). Join seven of first pieced blocks to form one vertical panel (top to bottom; see Diagram A). Repeat for two more panels. Join second set of pieced blocks to form three vertical panels in the same manner. Assemble panels as shown in Diagram A, then join seams from top to bottom, matching horizontal seams. Press seams open.

Making inner border — Join shorter red print strips to top and bottom of assembled pieced blocks and longer ones to sides, including ends of top and bottom inner border sections.

Making outer border — Join shorter strips to top and bottom of inner border and longer ones to sides, including ends of top and bottom outer border sections.

Run contrast basting threads centered lengthwise (continuation of vertical center seam) and crosswise on quilt (see Diagram A).

Note: Quilt may be made wider or longer by adding borders at sides, top and bottom or both.

Backing and interlining — Cut three 2¾ yard lengths of fabric for backing. Remove selvages. Join together lengthwise, taking ¼" seams. You should have a piece about 99" long and 104" wide. Trim away 8½" from side edges and ¾" from one end or so that backing and quilt top are the same size. Turn under ¼" on all edges of each piece separately; baste. Place quilt backing flat on floor, wrong side up; smooth it out. Place quilt batting on top, one strip next to another without overlapping, if piecing is necessary. Lay the quilt top in place, right side up; pin all three layers together, edges even. Starting at center of quilt, with contrast thread, baste through all layers out to midpoint of all four edges; next, baste from center to corners. Baste outer edges together.

Marking the quilt design — This may be done before or after putting the quilt into the frame. Simple patterns (such as the straight lines on inner border and pieced blocks) can be drawn directly on the quilt with pencil and ruler (see Diagram B). On outer border, run a contrast basting thread along center of strip to mark center of design. It is advisable to try out design on tracing paper before marking quilt. Mark one corner and about two motifs each side as indicated by broken lines on Diagram B; use ruler and a cup or plate as a guide. Trace design on fabric lightly with a pencil.

Quilting — Use quilting frame or a large hoop (22" or more in diameter) to hold the fabric taut while it is being quilted.

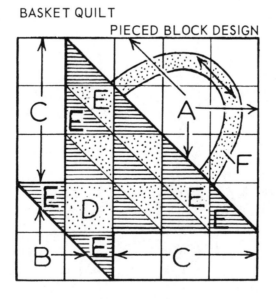

BASKET QUILT
PIECED BLOCK DESIGN

BASKET QUILT

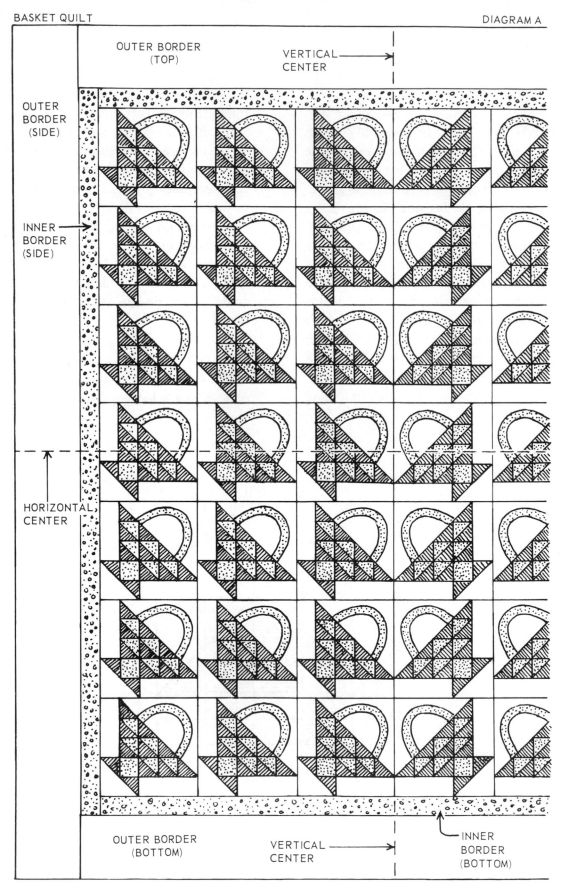

90

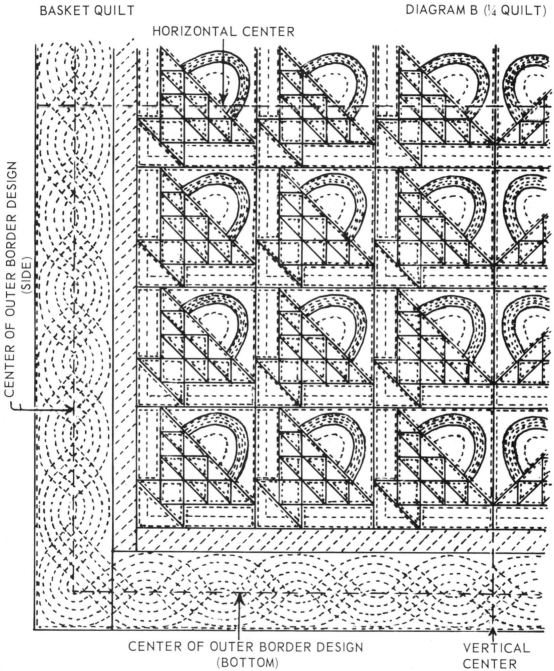

HORIZONTAL CENTER

CENTER OF OUTER BORDER DESIGN
(SIDE)

CENTER OF OUTER BORDER DESIGN
(BOTTOM)

VERTICAL
CENTER

EIGHT POINTED STAR CRIB QUILT

(continued from page 31)

DIRECTIONS: From white, cut two lengths 6" by 32" and two 6" by 17 3/8" for border; using patterns given, cut 48 squares and 48 triangles for outside of star block. From blue, cut two long strips 2" x 23" and nine short strips 2" x 5" for setting blocks together. From prints and solids, using pattern given, cut 96 diamond shaped pieces for star motifs. Reserve remaining blue fabric for binding. (When ready to bind, cut 1½" wide strips, piecing as needed to fit around quilt.)

Making a star block — Right sides together, join eight assorted diamond shaped pieces to form a star as shown. Join white squares and white triangles to star between points to form a block (see Diagram). Continue in this manner until all diamonds, squares and triangles are used and 12 star blocks have been completed.

Assembling center star block panel — Right sides together, join a short blue strip to one side of a star block. Join another star block to opposite side of blue strip. Continue in this manner until you have a strip of four star blocks separated by three blue strips. Using remaining star blocks and short blue strips, make two more strips in same way. Now join a star block strip to a long blue strip and continue until there are three star block strips separated by two blue strips. Center panel is now complete (see diagram of center panel).

Finishing — Taking ½" seams, join short border pieces to short ends of center panel, then join long border pieces to sides. Finish quilt according to General Instructions.

Note: Actual size quilting pattern is given. See also the corner detail for joining seams of border.

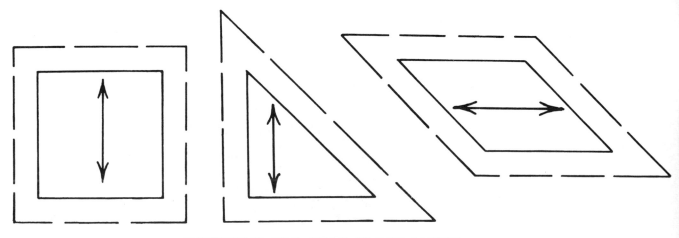

PATTERNS FOR STAR BLOCK MOTIF

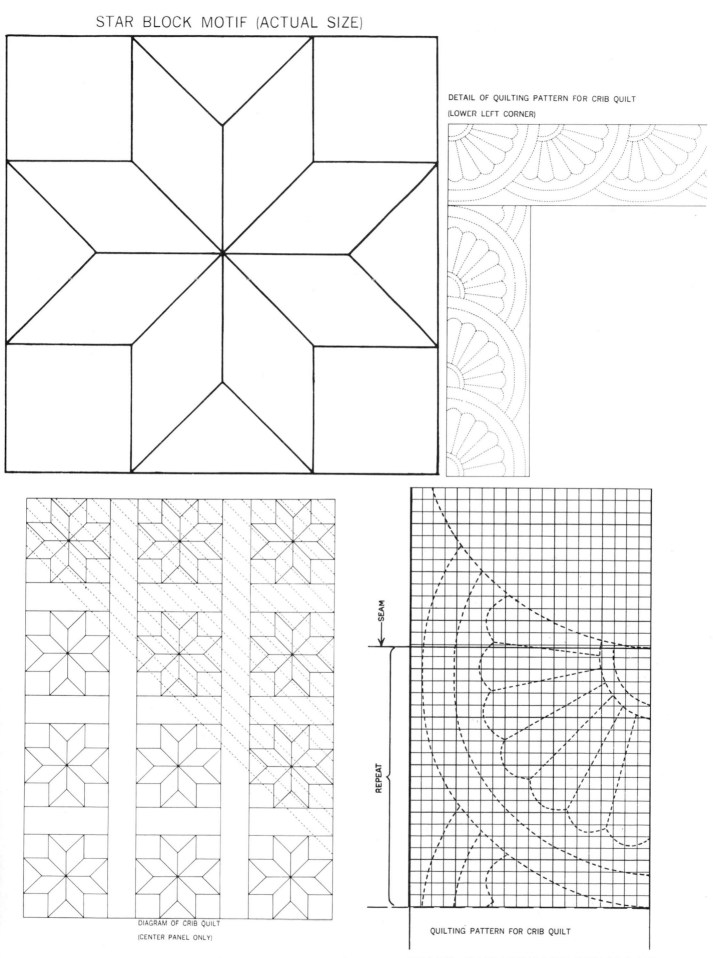

STAR BLOCK MOTIF (ACTUAL SIZE)

DETAIL OF QUILTING PATTERN FOR CRIB QUILT
(LOWER LEFT CORNER)

DIAGRAM OF CRIB QUILT
(CENTER PANEL ONLY)

SEAM

REPEAT

QUILTING PATTERN FOR CRIB QUILT

SCALE: EACH SQUARE EQUALS ½"

93

VARIABLE STAR QUILT
(continued from page 32)

MATERIALS:

36" wide fine percale or
  broadcloth —
1¾ yards white
14½ yards blue (includes
  backing and binding)
Thin cotton or synthetic
  batting for interlining
Quilting thread
Short needle

DIRECTIONS: (To enlarge pattern see page 15. Make a durable pattern from cardboard.)

Cutting fabric — From white fabric, cut 48 squares 5¾" by 5¾"; also 48 triangles using cardboard pattern, placing arrow on straight grain of fabric. From blue fabric, cut 12 squares 5¾" by 5¾", 144 triangles cut by pattern same as above, also two side borders and two panels — each 6½" by 91", two end borders 6½" by 71¾" and nine joining strips, each 6½" by 16¼". Cut 1¼" wide straight strips for binding.

Diagram A shows quilt containing 12 pieced blocks connected by nine crosswise joining strips and two vertical panels, with 6½" borders and 3/8" binding.

Assembling quilt — Join units of pieced blocks according to Design Chart, working from the centers out. With right sides together and using fine running stitches, take exact ¼" seams; start and stop at seam lines at corners. Be careful not to stretch bias edges. Press seams as you go.

Join four pieced blocks and three joining strips, end to end (see Diagram A), taking up ¼" seam allowance. Repeat two more times.

Next, join two vertical panels and two side borders to above pieces, then end borders to top and bottom, including ends of side borders (see Diagram A).

Marking quilting pattern — Using ruler as a guide, mark lines lightly with pencil between corners on each plain square of pieced blocks, continuing lines into side and end borders. Mark lines on borders and panels parallel and at right angle to these lines, 1¾" apart. Pieced blocks are quilted next to seams (Diagram B.)

Backing and interlining — Cut two lengths for backing slightly longer than quilt. Remove selvages and stitch width of fabric together lengthwise; add any required width at sides. The backing should be a little larger than pieced top. Use quilt batting (sold in a variety of sizes) for interlining. Lay the quilt backing flat on floor, wrong side up; smooth it out. Place quilt batting on top, one strip next to another without overlapping, if piecing is necessary. Lay the quilt top in place, right side up; pin all three layers together. Starting at center of quilt, baste out to midpoint of all four edges; next, baste from center to corners. Baste outer edges together.

Quilting — Use quilting frame or a large hoop (22" or more in diameter) to hold the fabric taut while it is being quilted.

Finishing — Join strips for binding, end to end, to fit around entire quilt; press seams open. Join one edge of binding to quilt, right sides together, taking ¼" seam, pleating at corners to miter. Turn in ¼" on free edge and hem over seam on underside.

PIECED BLOCK DESIGN

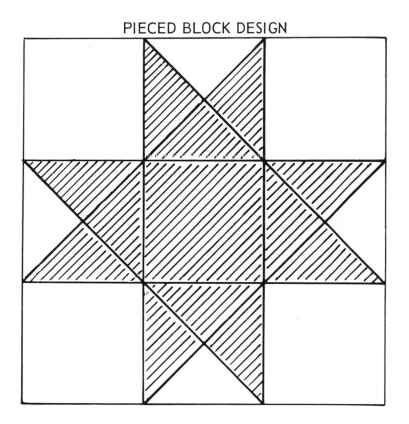

PATTERN FOR TRIANGLE

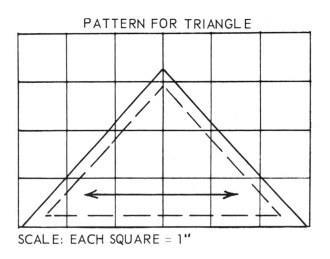

SCALE: EACH SQUARE = 1"

VARIABLE STAR QUILT

DIAGRAM A

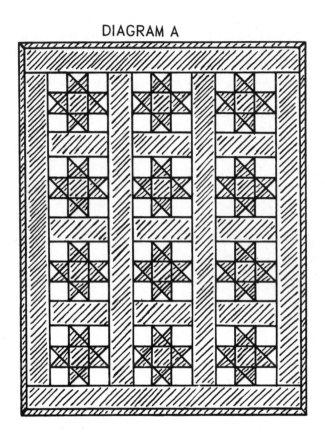

DIAGRAM B (¼ QUILT)

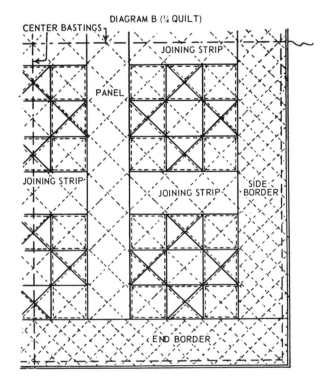

KEEPSAKE QUILT

(continued from page 65)

The elegant and unusual Keepsake Quilt is interesting because of the elaborate bouquet motifs used throughout. There are no two alike. Much of the applique is padded or gathered into petals and rosettes. On some blocks the berries are stuffed, giving a three dimensional effect. Many colors and fabrics have been used. It would be impossible to give instructions for copying the quilt exactly so we are here giving patterns for four of the bouquets for those who wish to make a similar quilt.

The quilt shown in the photograph is about 78" wide and 68" from top to bottom — an unusual size, which indicates it was never finished. We give instructions for a quilt 95" by 95", consisting of 13 appliqued blocks (repeating four designs adapted from the original quilt), 12 alternating plain blocks (to be quilted in design given) and 5" appliqued borders all around (see Diagram A). The large center

design on the original quilt was too intricate for a pattern to be given. The finished size of the quilt may be varied to fit the requirements of your bed by increasing or decreasing the number of blocks in length or width and omitting top, bottom or side borders. A corresponding change will have to be made in materials required.

MATERIALS:

9 yards 36" wide white fabric
  (with a firm weave, but soft
  texture, such as fine percale
  or broadcloth)
36" wide percale or broadcloth:
2 yards dark green calico print (A)
½ yard plain leaf green (B)
5/8 yard plain turkey red (C)
¼ yard plain dark brown (D)
¾ yard plain light brown (E)
¼ yard yellow calico print (F)
½ yard plain light blue (G)
¼ yard plain light pink (H)
¼ yard red-orange (J)
Thin cotton or synthetic quilt
  batting for interlining,
  available in a variety of sizes,
  enough to cover 95" by 95"
  area, pieced without overlapping

DIAGRAM A

TOP BORDER		
1	2	3
4	1	
2	3	4
1	2	
3	4	1

SIDE BORDER (left) · SIDE BORDER (right)

LOWER BORDER

1-2-3-4—APPLIQUÉD BLOCKS

KEEPSAKE QUILT

8¼ yards 36" wide unstarched
white fabric similar in texture
to the top for backing
Good 6-cord No. 50 or 60 white
mercerized cotton thread, if
joining blocks by hand; No. 70
if done by machine.
For all hand applique work, use
No. 70 in matching colors
Quilting thread and a short needle
for quilting
6-strand embroidery cotton
in colors indicated in Color
Key for all block designs
Stuffing for berries and cherries —
cotton balls (or left-over quilt
batting)

DIRECTIONS: Making patterns — Trace each pattern exactly onto tracing paper, then cut a more durable pattern from brown paper or lightweight cardboard. Indicate on each pattern the color letter and number of times each unit is to be cut.

Cutting fabric — Press fabric thoroughly, making certain crosswise threads are squared with the selvage; use a damp cloth (or steam iron) if necessary to remove wrinkles. Trim away all selvages.

Top of quilt: Cut 25 squares, each 17½" by 17½". Cut two strips for side borders, each 6" by 96" and two for top and lower borders, each 6" by 86". For appliques, place long thin patterns (tree trunks, branches, flower stems, etc.) on lengthwise grain. For smaller irregular pieces, the grain does not matter.

Trace around pattern the number of times required, using best layout possible to save fabric, then cut. (Note: 1/8" has been allowed on edges of appliques for turn-under, except where inner curves and corners are too narrow. At these places, slash on solid lines and turn under on broken lines). Group together pieces of a kind; where there are many, run a thread through centers to hold until needed.

KEY FOR ALL BLOCK DESIGNS
Fabric Appliques, Berries, Cherries:

A — Dark green calico print
B — Plain leaf green
C — Plain turkey red
D — Plain dark brown
E — Plain light brown
F — Yellow calico print
G — Plain light blue
H — Plain light pink
J — Plain red-orange

Embroidery:

Color	Stitch
1. Dark Green	a. Chain stitch
2. Turquoise	b. Straight stitch
3. Dark brown	c. Running stitch
4. Yellow	d. Outline stitch
5. Turkey red	e. Blanket stitch
6. Light brown	f. French knot
7. Light green	g. Feather stitch

Marking block design — Trace design onto tracing paper, including outer solid line. Pin tracing to 17½" square of fabric, ¼" seam allowance extending beyond outer solid line on all edges. Using dressmaker's carbon and sharp pencil, trace main units onto block — tree trunk, branches, stems, leaves and larger units. The smaller units may be positioned by reference to Design Chart.

Preparing appliques — You will require four repeats of Design No. 1 and three repeats of Designs No. 2, 3 and 4. Turn under 1/8" allowance on all units required for design you are working on, including two "J" circles on Design No. 3, but excepting all other circles and rectangles — these will be cherries, berries, yo-yos and gathered petals or flowers with special instructions to follow. Clip inner curves and corners where necessary for smooth turning; press. Edges where no turn-under is indicated on pattern will be covered by units with turned edges.

Making yo-yos: Turn under 1/8" on edges of circle, then gather close to fold, using thread doubled in needle. Draw up gathers as closely as possible, fasten securely (see Detail).

YO-YO

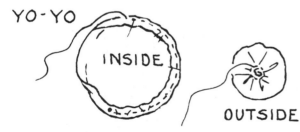

Making cherries and berries: Turn under 1/8" on edges and gather as for yo-yos, stuff firmly with small amount of cotton or quilt batting. Draw up gathers, fasten securely (see Detail).

CHERRY OR BERRY   STUFFING

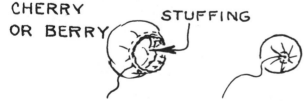

Making gathered petals: Fold circle in half on true bias of fabric. Using thread doubled in needle, gather 1/8" from edges to fit size indicated on Design Chart; some petals are drawn up closer than others; fasten threads (see Detail).

GATHERED PETALS

BIAS

On block design No. 4, there is no pattern given for the tubular petals on the center flower. Cut four G pieces, each 2" by 1¾"; join 2" sides, taking 1/8" seams. Press seams open, turn. With seam at center, gather top end 1/8" from edges; draw into ¼", fasten. Gathered ends are sewn to position under yo-yo on Design, lower ends under gathered petals.

Making gathered flowers: Seam ends of rectangles, taking up 1/8" seam. Press seam open, turn. Fold in half, raw edges even, gather 1/8" from edges. Draw up gathers tightly, fasten securely (see Detail).

GATHERED FLOWERS

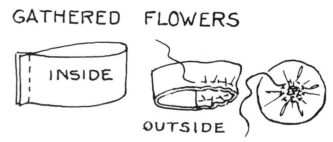

INSIDE

OUTSIDE

KEEPSAKE QUILT

Making applique and embroidering blocks — Pin each unit of design in place as shown on Design Chart, matching colors and covering raw edges carefully. Sew on flat units first, with invisible hemming stitches in matching thread, barely catching the edge of each unit and keeping its true shape. Embroider, following Key for Colors and Stitches. Use full six strands of cotton for bold effect, 2 or 3 strands for more delicate details.

Marking and placing applique on borders — Trace border design onto tracing paper. Pin tracing along each border, overlapping tissue to dotted line for continuous repeat of design; mark with pins at each repetition to determine number of repeats necessary for each section to end with whole leaves. Border must be planned so that leaves run around entire quilt border in same direction. Adjust to fit, if necessary, before tracing design on borders as for block designs. Applique leaves are same as flat units on block designs. Cut out an equal number of yo-yos from A and C fabric scraps. Make and sew to borders between leaves according to design, alternating colors.

EMBROIDERY STITCH DETAILS

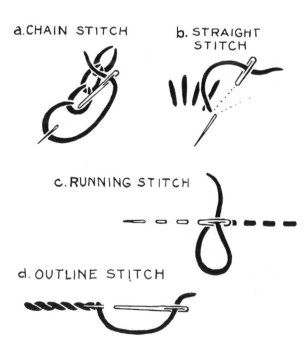

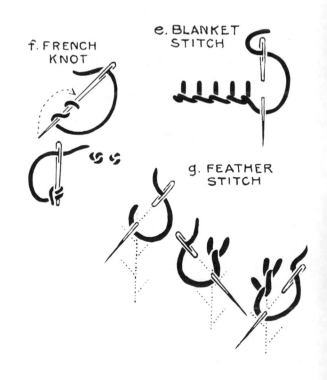

DIAGRAM FOR BLOCK DESIGN NO. 1 (17" SQUARE)

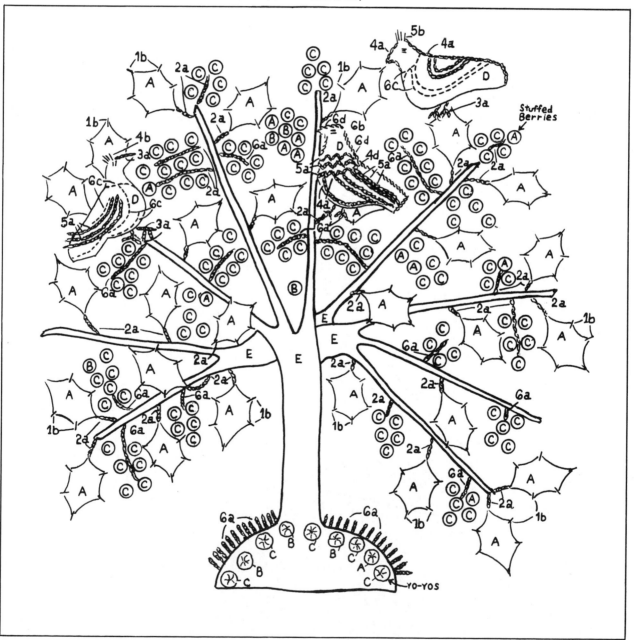

KEEPSAKE QUILT

PATTERNS FOR BLOCK DESIGN NO. 1

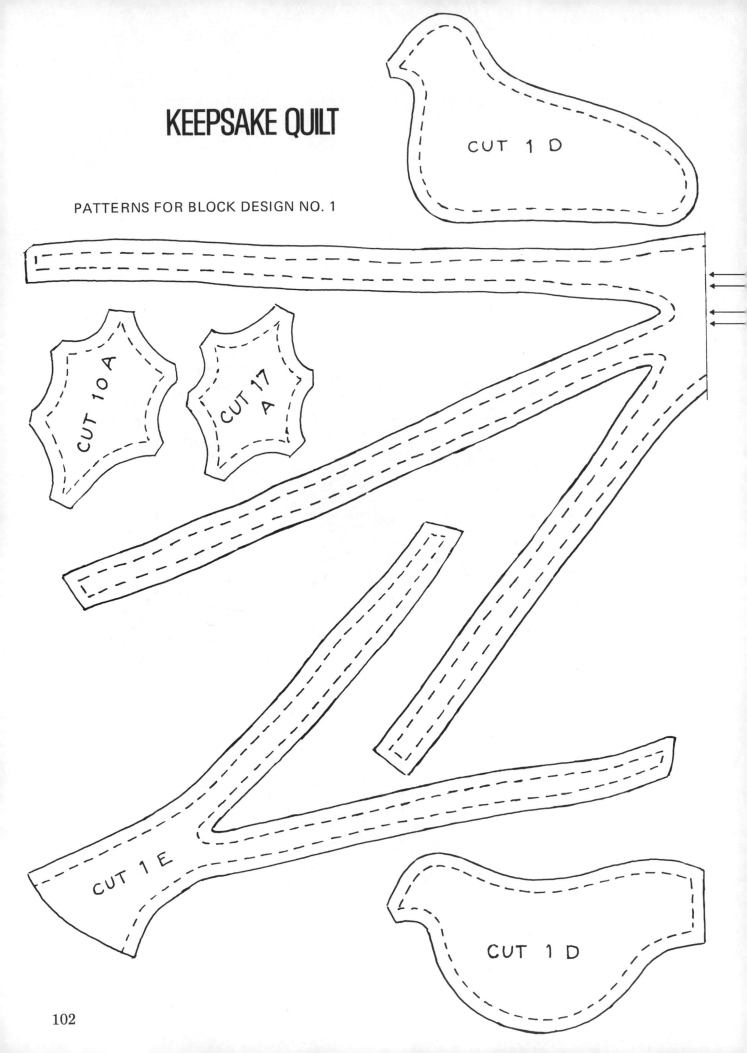

CUT 1 D

CUT 10 A

CUT 17 A

CUT 1 E

CUT 1 D

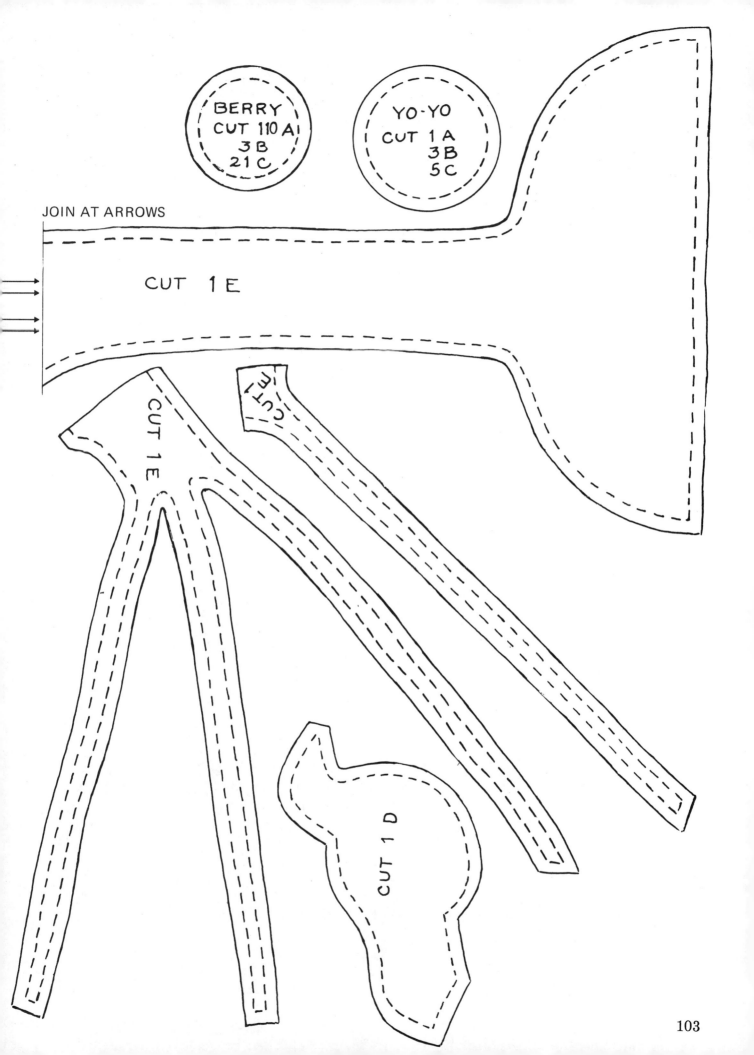

BERRY
CUT 110 A
3 B
21 C

YO-YO
CUT 1 A
3 B
5 C

JOIN AT ARROWS

CUT 1 E

CUT 1 E

CUT 1 E

CUT 1 D

KEEPSAKE QUILT

DIAGRAM FOR BLOCK DESIGN NO. 2 (17″ SQUARE)

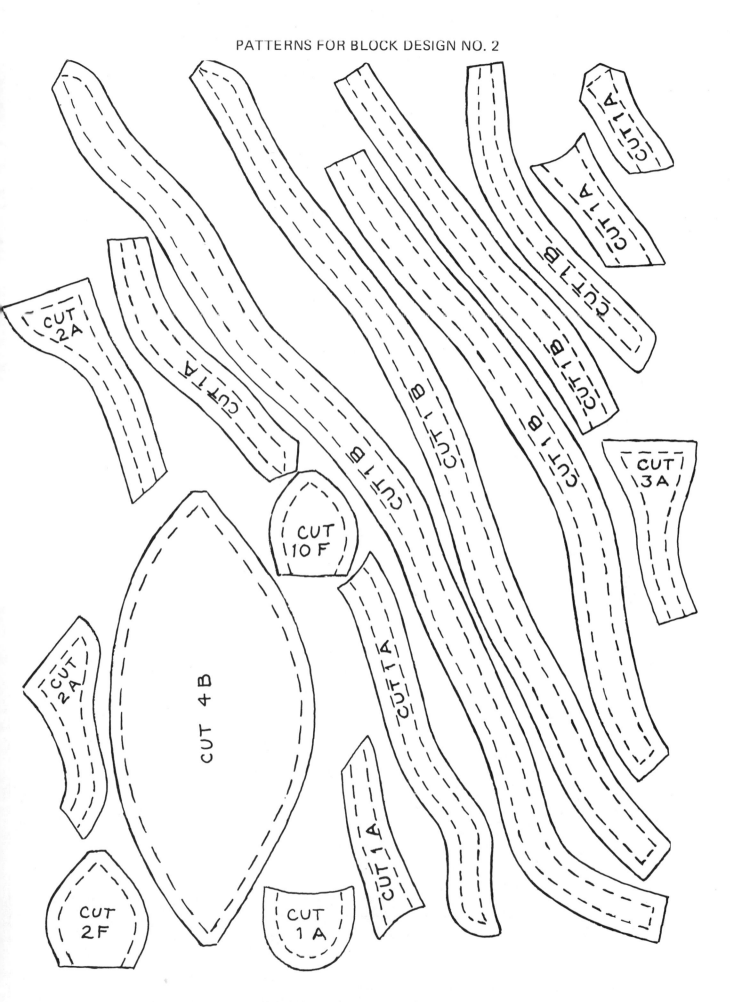

KEEPSAKE QUILT

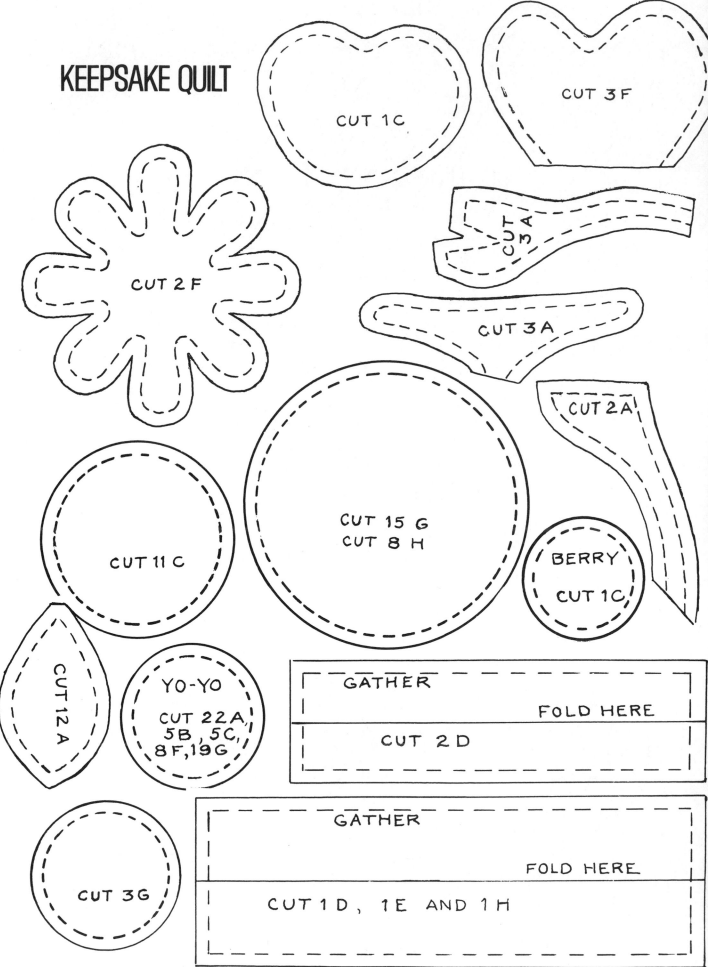

CUT 1 C

CUT 3 F

CUT 3 A

CUT 3 A

CUT 2 F

CUT 2 A

CUT 11 C

CUT 15 G
CUT 8 H

BERRY
CUT 1 C

CUT 12 A

YO-YO
CUT 22 A,
5 B, 5 C,
8 F, 19 G

GATHER
FOLD HERE
CUT 2 D

GATHER
FOLD HERE
CUT 1 D, 1 E AND 1 H

CUT 3 G

DIAGRAM FOR BLOCK DESIGN NO. 3 (17″ SQUARE)

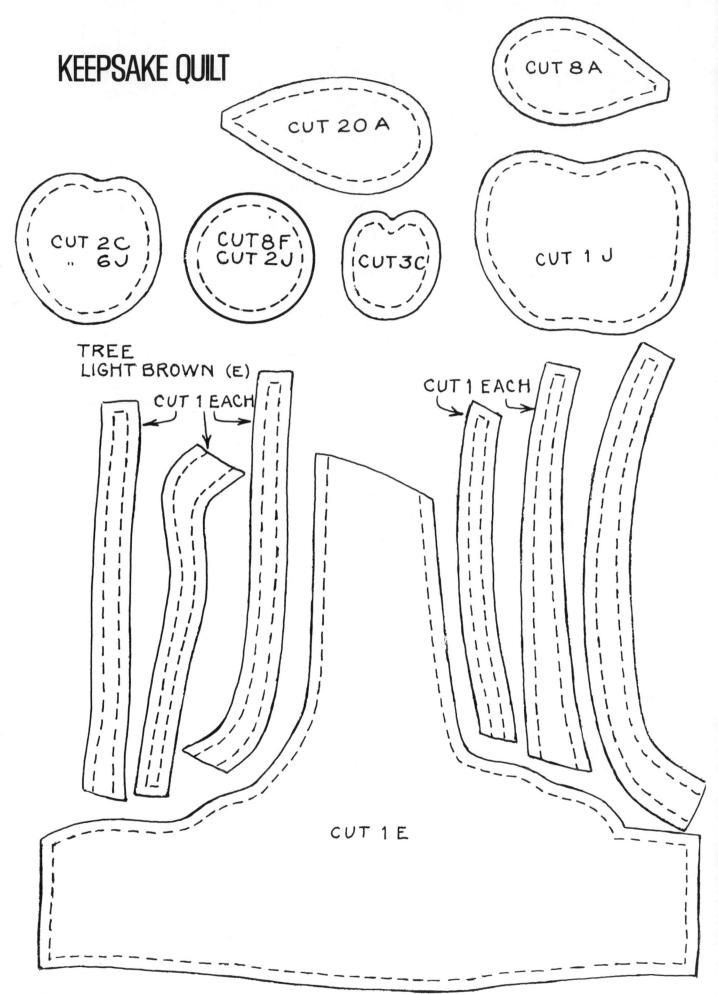

KEEPSAKE QUILT

CUT 8 A

CUT 20 A

CUT 2C
6J

CUT 8F
CUT 2J

CUT 3C

CUT 1 J

TREE
LIGHT BROWN (E)

CUT 1 EACH

CUT 1 EACH

CUT 1 E

PATTERNS FOR BLOCK DESIGN NO. 3

DIAGRAM FOR BLOCK DESIGN NO. 4 (17" SQUARE)

KEEPSAKE QUILT

PATTERNS FOR BLOCK DESIGN NO. 4

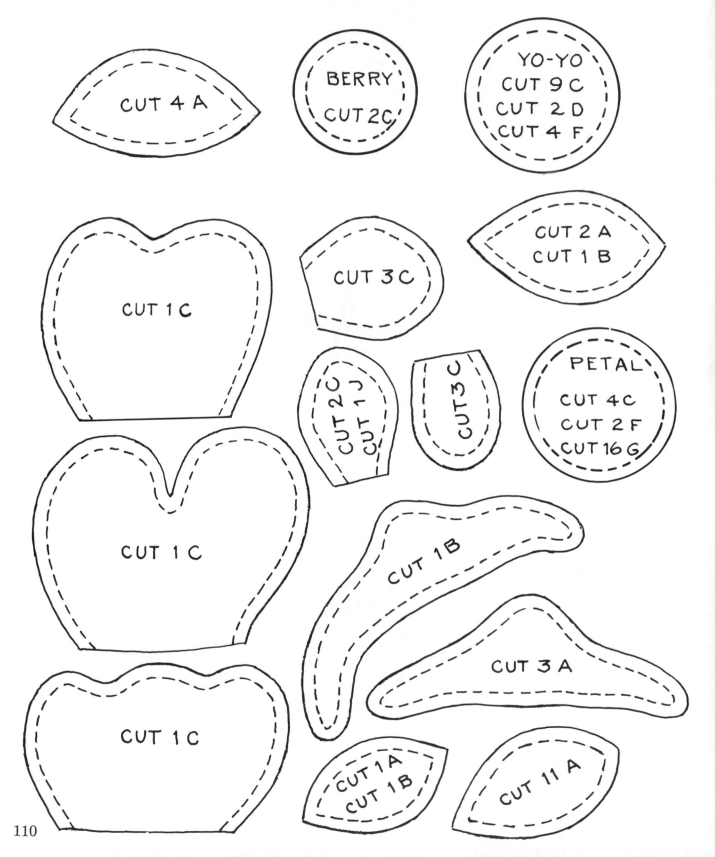

CUT 4 A

BERRY
CUT 2C

YO-YO
CUT 9 C
CUT 2 D
CUT 4 F

CUT 1 C

CUT 3 C

CUT 2 A
CUT 1 B

CUT 1 C

CUT 2 C
CUT 1 J

CUT 3 C

PETAL
CUT 4 C
CUT 2 F
CUT 16 G

CUT 1 C

CUT 1 B

CUT 3 A

CUT 1 A
CUT 1 B

CUT 11 A

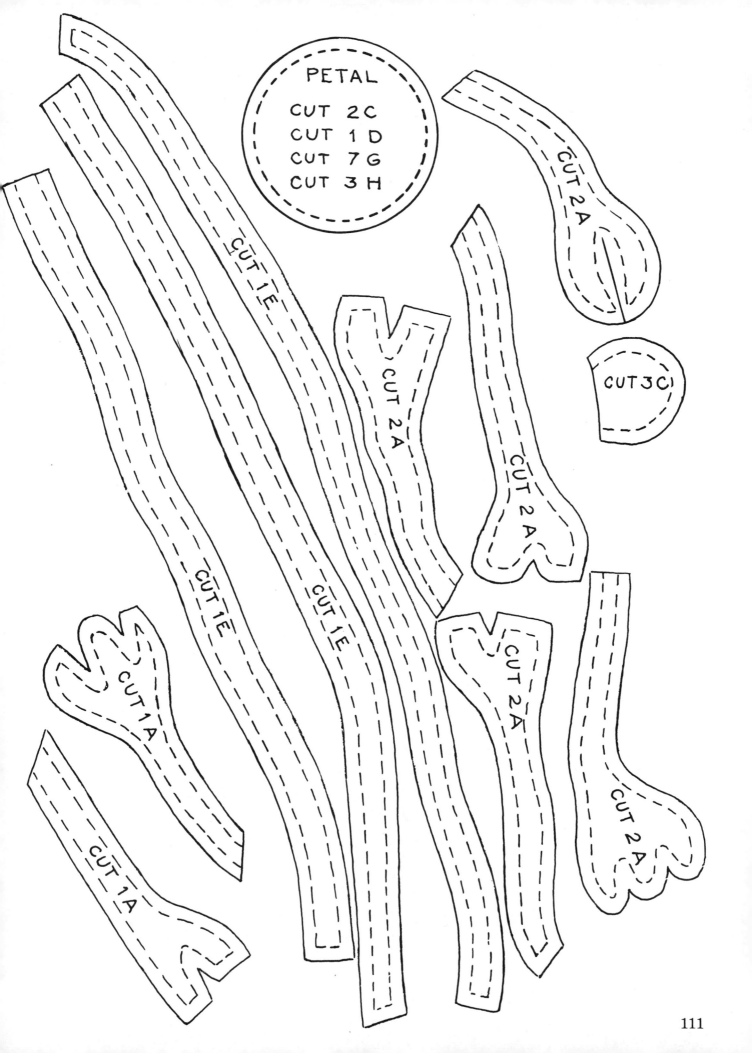

PETAL

CUT 2C
CUT 1 D
CUT 7 G
CUT 3 H

CUT 2A

CUT 3C

CUT 1E

CUT 1E

CUT 1E

CUT 1E

CUT 2A

CUT 2A

CUT 2A

CUT 1A

CUT 1A

CUT 2A

KEEPSAKE QUILT

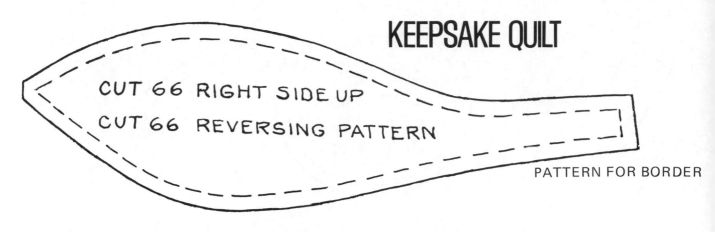

CUT 66 RIGHT SIDE UP

CUT 66 REVERSING PATTERN

PATTERN FOR BORDER

DIAGRAM FOR BORDER PLACEMENT— AREA REPRESENTS 17" x 5"

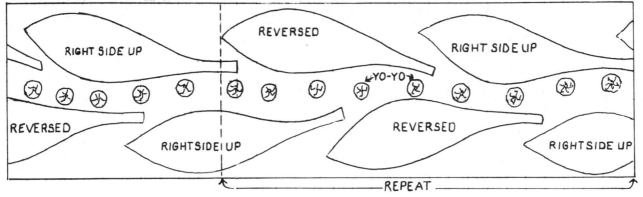

RIGHT SIDE UP

REVERSED

RIGHT SIDE UP

REVERSED

RIGHTSIDE UP

YO-YO

REVERSED

RIGHTSIDE UP

REPEAT

DIAGRAM FOR THE
QUILTING OF PLAIN BLOCKS

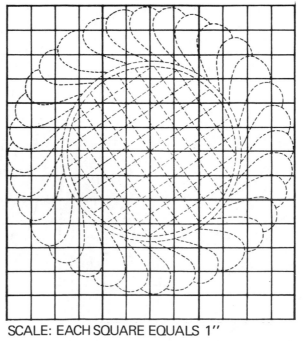

SCALE: EACH SQUARE EQUALS 1"

PRINCESS FEATHER QUILT

(continued from page 67)

DIRECTIONS: Appliqued center: Cut two 2 yard lengths of white fabric; remove selvages, then join long edges, right sides together, taking ¼" seam (center seam); press seam open. Run contrast basting across center at right angles to seam, then fold diagonally and run contrast bastings through center from corner to corner (see Diagram page 121).

MOTIF A

Cut applique units according to patterns and General Instructions. Turn under seam allowance (indicated by broken lines on pattern), slashing along solid lines between deep inner curves (unit 1 of Motif A and unit 10 of Motif B) and clipping inner curves and corners where indicated and outer curves where necessary; press (Detail a).

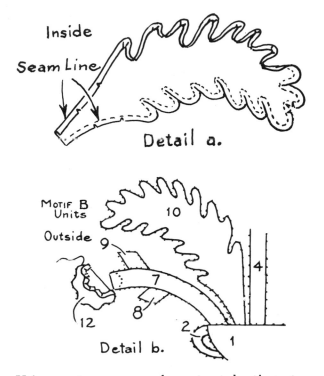

Detail a.

Detail b.

Using center seam and contrast bastings to align motifs, pin units in place as shown in Diagram; dotted lines on patterns are lapping lines; lap stems over leaves, flowers over stems (Detail b). For Motif B, lap unit 1 over 2, 3, 4, 7 and 10; place raw edges of top, bottom and side center units 1 even with edges of quilt center; turn under lower edges of remaining units 1 and place 8½" from corners. Sew on with invisible hemming stitches (using matching thread), barely catching the edge of each unit and keeping its true shape. (Note: Broken lines in center of patterns for unit 3 of Motif A and units 1 and 10 of Motif B are quilting lines to be worked later.)

PRINCESS FEATHER QUILT

Making patchwork border — Join units according to "Piecing" under General Instructions, making two strips with 17 square motifs for top and bottom sections and two strips with 19 square motifs for side sections. Press whole strips carefully after they have been set together. Pin shorter strips to top and bottom of appliqued center, right sides together, ends even. Stitch ¼" seams; press open. Pin and stitch longer strips to side edges of appliqued center and ends of top and bottom patchwork borders in same manner.

Making outer border — Trim selvages from remaining 5¼ yards of white fabric. Cut two pieces 15" by 78" for top and bottom; two pieces 15" by 108" for sides. Join top and bottom to patchwork border, right sides together, taking ¼" seams; press seams open. Join side sections to patchwork border and ends of top and bottom outer borders in same manner.

Marking quilt pattern — See General Instructions. For Motif A, trace following Quilting Design for flower between each unit 1 as shown in Diagram-Design for Quilting. For background quilting, mark squares 1 1/8" apart on appliqued center, also at corners and along inner edges of outer border. Starting at center of top outer border and continuing around to center of bottom outer border, mark ovals forming central unit of design about 8" wide by 10½" long; mark plume design and 2" diameter circles as in Diagram. Repeat in reverse for opposite side.

Backing, batting and quilting — See General Instructions. Starting at center, first quilt circles on unit 3 of Motif A, then flower motifs between each unit 1. Next, quilt 1/8" inside and outside each applique piece and quilting lines on units 1 and 10 of Motif B. Quilt 1/8" each side of each seam in patchwork border, then plume design and background squares on outer border.

Finishing — Bind edges with white fabric, or, trim batting and backing 3/8" from outer edges, turn quilt top edges to underside and hem to backing.

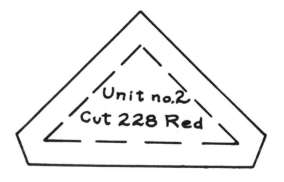

PATTERNS FOR PATCHWORK BORDER

114

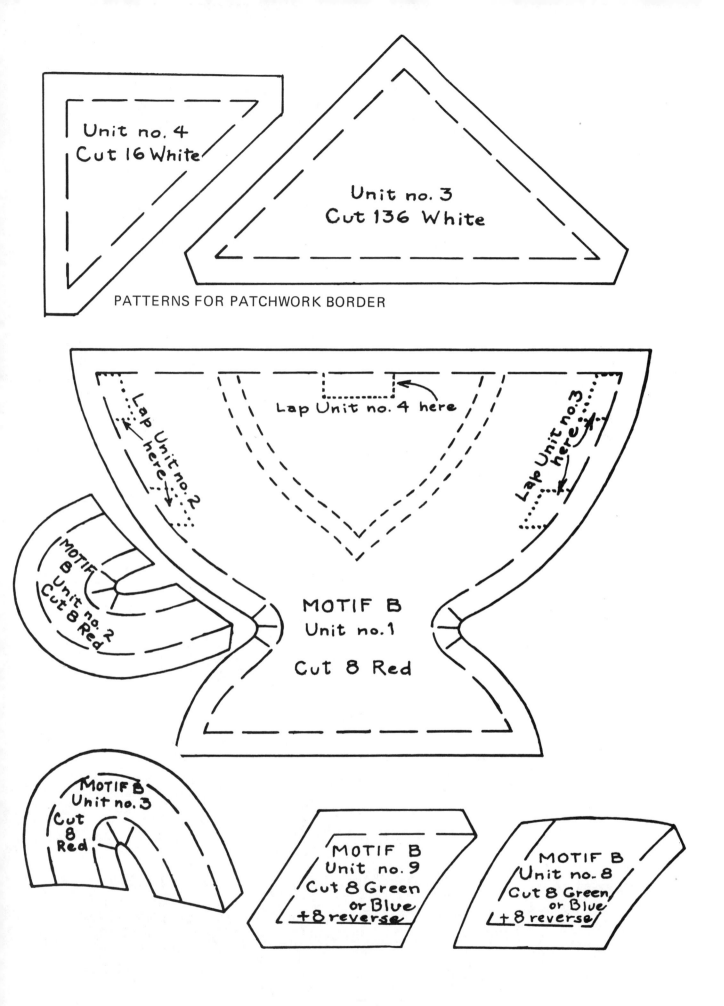

Unit no. 4
Cut 16 White

Unit no. 3
Cut 136 White

PATTERNS FOR PATCHWORK BORDER

Lap Unit no. 4 here

Lap Unit no. 2 here

Lap Unit no. 3 here

MOTIF B
Unit no. 2
Cut 8 Red

MOTIF B
Unit no. 1

Cut 8 Red

MOTIF B
Unit no. 3
Cut 8 Red

MOTIF B
Unit no. 9
Cut 8 Green
or Blue
+8 reverse

MOTIF B
Unit no. 8
Cut 8 Green
or Blue
+8 reverse

PATTERNS

PRINCESS FEATHER QUILT

PATTERNS

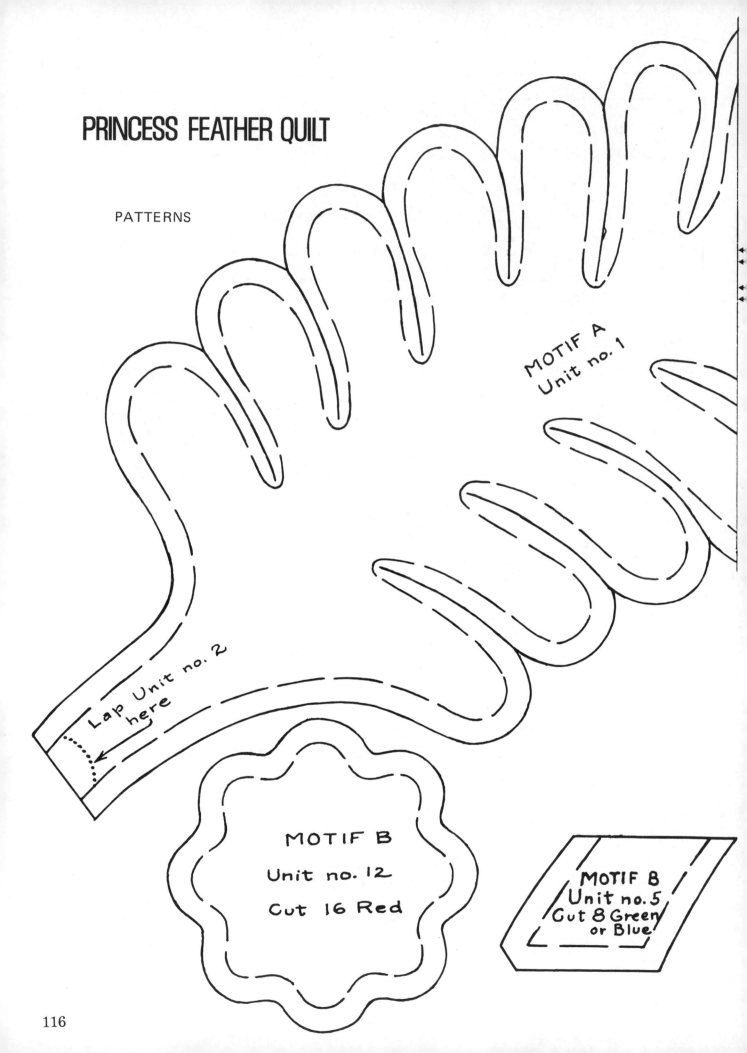

MOTIF A
Unit no. 1

Lap Unit no. 2
here

MOTIF B

Unit no. 12

Cut 16 Red

MOTIF B
Unit no. 5
Cut 8 Green
or Blue

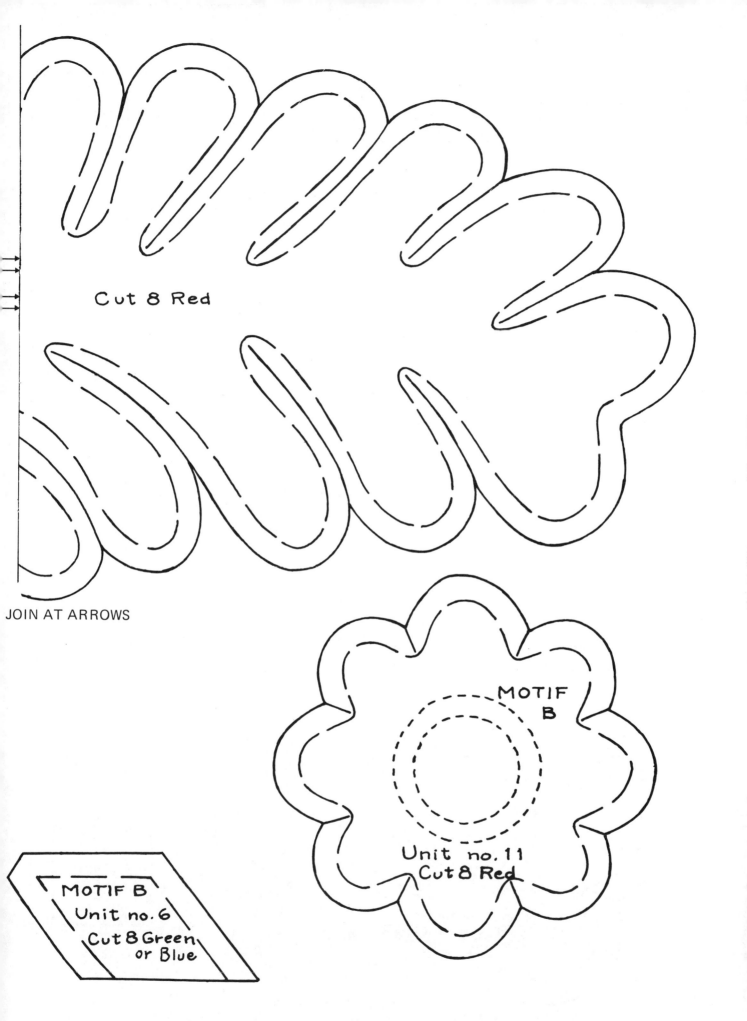

Cut 8 Red

JOIN AT ARROWS

MOTIF
B

Unit no. 11
Cut 8 Red

MOTIF B
Unit no. 6
Cut 8 Green
or Blue

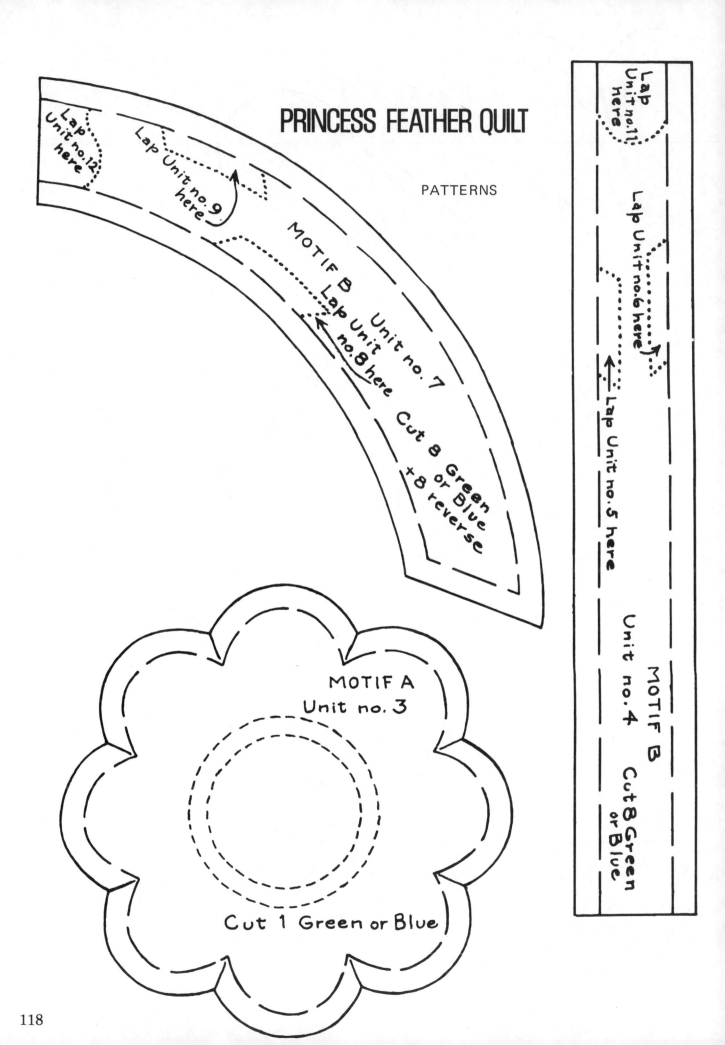

PRINCESS FEATHER QUILT

PATTERNS

Lap Unit no.12 here

Lap Unit no. 9 here

MOTIF B Unit no. 7

Lap Unit no.8 here

Cut 8 Green or Blue +8 reverse

MOTIF A
Unit no. 3

Cut 1 Green or Blue

Lap Unit no.11 here

Lap Unit no.6 here

Lap Unit no.5 here

MOTIF B
Unit no. 4   Cut 8 Green or Blue

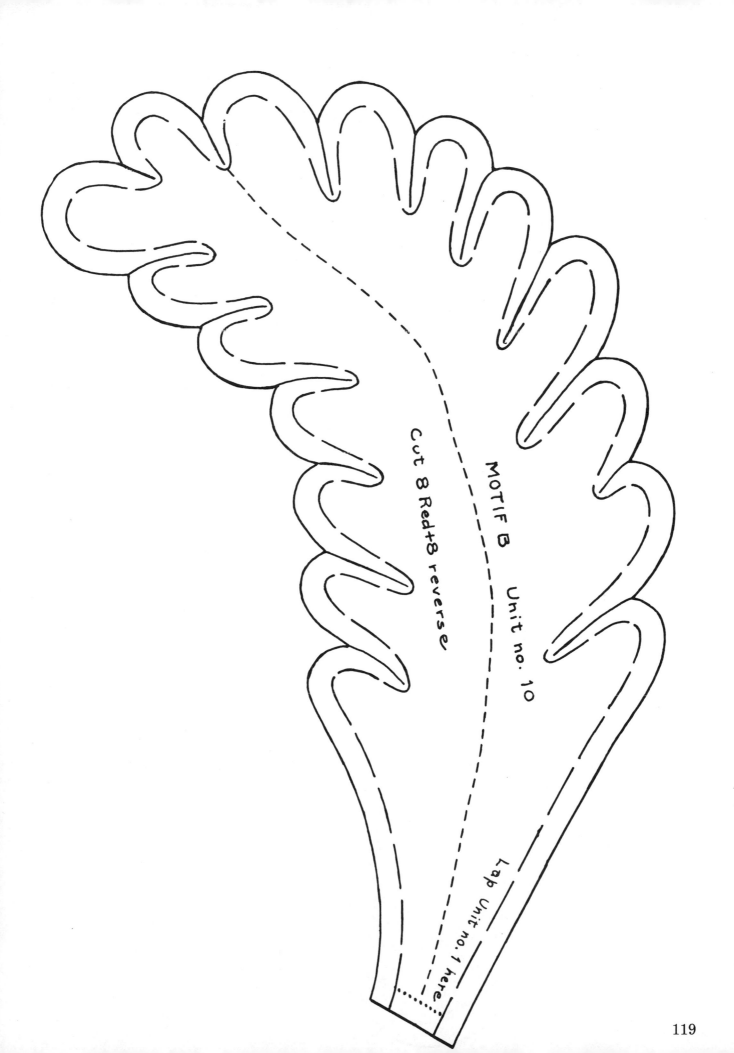

MOTIF B   Unit no. 10

Cut 8 Red+8 reverse

Lap Unit no.1 here

PRINCESS FEATHER QUILT

PATTERN

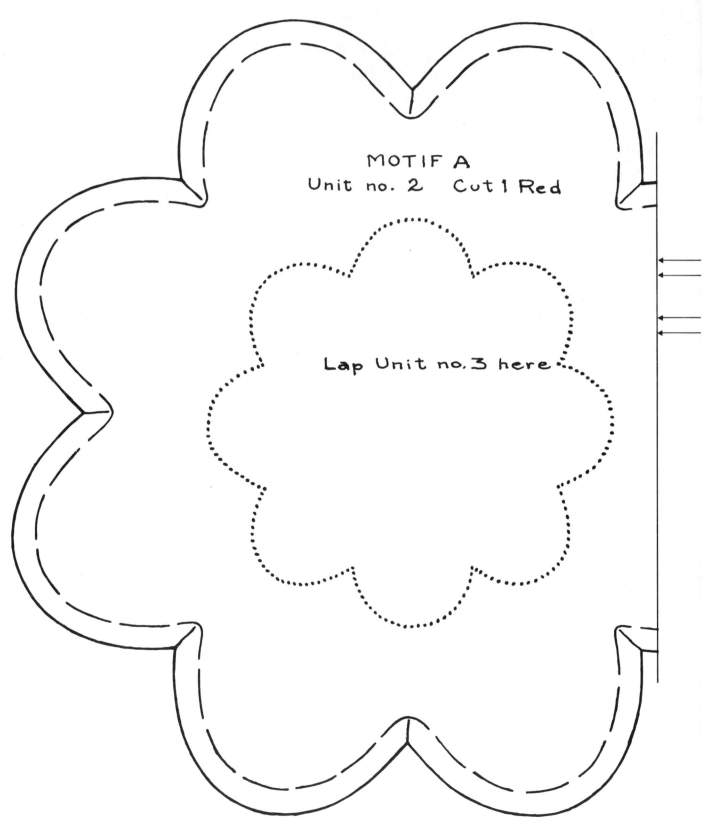

MOTIF A
Unit no. 2   Cut 1 Red

Lap Unit no. 3 here

JOIN AT ARROWS

OUTER BORDER
(TOP)

8½"

MOTIF B

MOTIF A
UNITS

CENTER SEAM

BASTING

OUTER
BORDER
(SIDE)

OUTER
BORDER
(SIDE)

MOTIF B
UNITS

PATCHWORK BORDER

OUTER BORDER
(BOTTOM)

¼ PLUME QUILT - DESIGN FOR QUILTING

CENTER OF SIDE BORDER

CENTER OF BOTTOM BORDER

121

DUTCH COUNTRY QUILT

(continued from page 68)

MATERIALS:

6 yards 44-45" wide purple fabric
with a firm weave, but soft
texture such as fine percale
or broadcloth

About ¼ yard each of different
small prints for appliques —

10 with red background (A to J)
except ½ yard for I

2 with black background (K and L)

3/8 yard plain turkey red (M)

Scrap of plain leaf green (N)

Turkey red bias tapes — 12
yards 1" wide and 8½ yards
single fold and 4 yards
double fold

Thin cotton or synthetic quilt
batting for interlining,
available in a variety of
sizes; purchase enough to
cover an area 86" by 105",
pieced without overlapping

6 yards 44-45" wide plain
colored fabric, such as thin
muslin, for backing

No. 70 mercerized cotton thread
in purple, leaf green, black
and red

Matching thread for quilting

Short needle for quilting

6-strand embroidery cotton,
leaf green for tulip stems
on border applique, black
for birds' beaks, eyes
and feet

DIRECTIONS: (Enlarge patterns where necessary.) Trace each applique motif and quilting design (¼, ½ or whole, as given) onto tracing paper. Do same with cutting patterns for applique pieces. (To make more durable cutting patterns, cut from heavy brown paper, indicating on each pattern the color letter and number of times each unit is to be cut.)

Making quilt top — Press fabric thoroughly, making certain crosswise threads are squared with the selvage; use a damp cloth (or steam iron) if necessary to remove wrinkles. Cut into two 3 yard lengths, drawing thread to cut on true grain of fabric; trim away selvages. Join lengthwise seam on machine, taking ¼" seam; press open. To mark center for placement, run a contrast basting thread horizontally across quilt top 49½" above lower front end.

Making inner applique and quilting design 1 — Pin pattern to lower left quarter of top, matching horizontal basting and vertical seam lines as indicated. Using dressmaker's carbon and sharp pencil, trace all lines onto fabric. Reverse pattern, repeat in upper left quarter (see Design Chart). Reverse design and trace onto fabric on right side of seam in same manner.

Making center applique — Pin pattern to left half of top with center line on seam and outer line of stem on placement marked above; trace. Reverse pattern, trace onto right half.

Making border applique — Pin pattern for lower front section to left half of quilt top, with edges of scallops just inside cut edge,

122

center on vertical seam. (See Design Chart.) Pin pattern for side section above lower front section, continuing design by matching broken lines and having scallops the same distance from side edge of fabric; trace onto fabric. Repeat three more times and a little more to reach top of quilt (see Design Chart). Repeat for right side of quilt, reversing patterns.

Making bolster applique — Pin pattern to left half of quilt top, center on vertical seam, lower point of center tulip 14" below top edge (see Design Chart); trace. Reverse pattern, trace on right half.

Quilting designs 2 and 3 — Pin and trace onto left half of quilt top as shown in Design Chart, placing design 2 about 14" from vertical seam and centering design 3 on horizontal basting line. Repeat for right half.

Cutting fabric for appliques — Press fabric thoroughly. Place durable pattern on fabric, long ones (such as leaves) on lengthwise grain; for irregular pieces, the grain does not matter. Trace around pattern the number of times required, using best layout possible to save fabric, then cut. (Note: ¼" turn-under on appliques indicated by broken lines; dotted lines are lapping lines.) Group together pieces of a kind; where there are many, run a thread through centers to hold until needed.

Making center, inner and bolster appliques — Stems: Pin double fold bias tape (wider half up) along double lines with single fold edge toward center of quilt top; lap ends ¼" over placements for applique units (see Diagram A). Open out tape (removing one pin at a

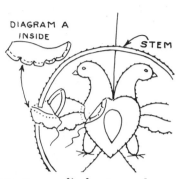

DIAGRAM A INSIDE

STEM

time as you proceed), baste under section in place. Machine (or hand) stitch to quilt top close to crease (see Detail a). Slipstitch outer edge of upper section flat to quilt top, using matching thread.

Detail a

DOUBLE FOLD BIAS TAPE

Making applique units — Turn under ¼" on edges indicated by broken lines, clipping inner curves and corners for smooth turning; press. Pin each unit of design in place as indicated, lapping turned edges to dotted lines where indicated; slipstitch to position, using matching thread (Diagram A). Using three strands of 6-strand black embroidery cotton in needle, work birds' eyes, beaks and feet in couching stitch (see Detail).

COUCHING STITCH

DUTCH COUNTRY QUILT

Making border applique — Stem: Pin single fold bias tape between inner double lines, easing it to fit flat on inward curves and stretching slightly on outward curves. When piecing is necessary, open out tape and join ends on straight grain of fabric; trim seam to ¼" and press open (see Detail b). Re-turn in edges, press. Carefully remove pins (one at a time), turn tape toward center (wrong side up) and baste inner cut edge in place, keeping crease along inner placement line. Machine or hand stitch close to crease. Turn bias outward (right side up) slipstitch free edge flat to quilt top (see Detail c).

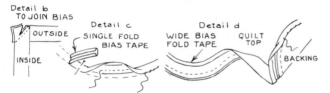

Remaining applique units: Prepare and slipstitch to position as for other appliques. Using full 6 strands of leaf green embroidery cotton in needle, work tulip stems in couching stitch.

Quilting — Work designs 1, 2 and 3 as marked. Next, quilt just outside each applique unit, then quilt background along marked lines (see Design Chart).

Binding edges of quilt — Trim all layers to 3/8" from outer basting line. Open out one fold edge of wide bias tape; pin, then baste crease along outer basting line, right sides together, at side and lower edges, raw edges outward. (Note: Piece tape same as for stem on border applique.) Machine stitch along crease (Detail d). Turn bias over edge, hem free edge over seam on backing side. Bind top edge in same manner, turning in ends.

PLACEMENT AND QUILTING PATTERN FOR BORDER APPLIQUE
SCALE: EACH SQUARE EQUALS 2"

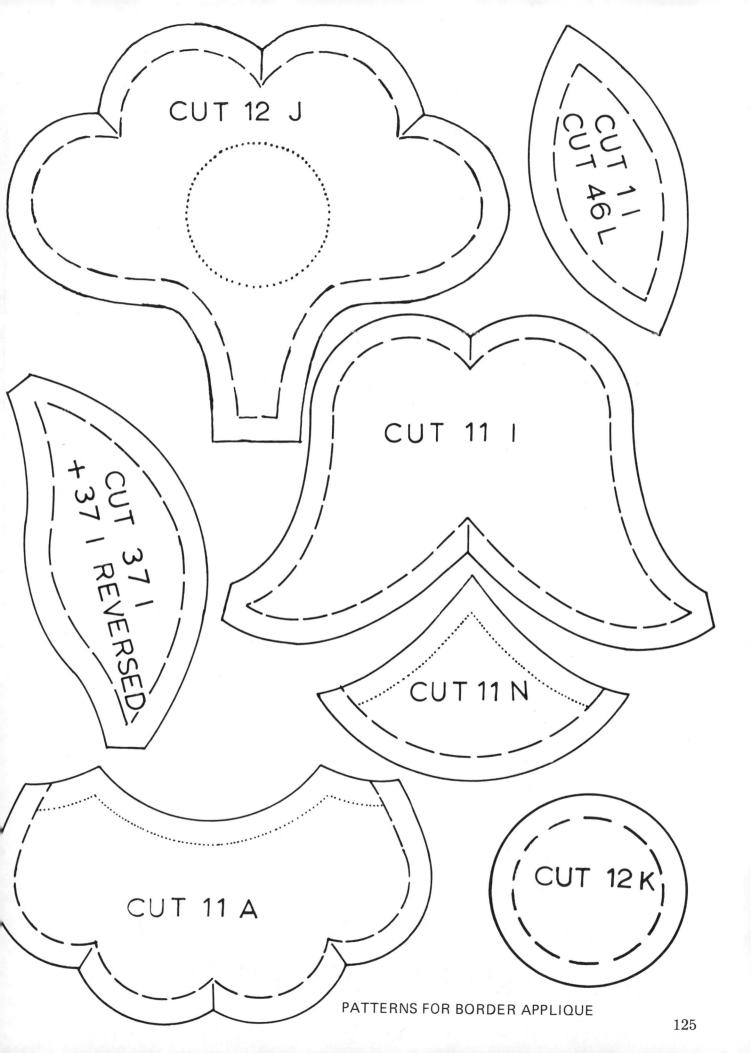

CUT 12 J

CUT 1 I
CUT 46 L

CUT 37 I
+ 37 I REVERSED

CUT 11 I

CUT 11 N

CUT 11 A

CUT 12 K

PATTERNS FOR BORDER APPLIQUE

DUTCH COUNTRY QUILT

PATTERNS FOR CENTER APPLIQUE

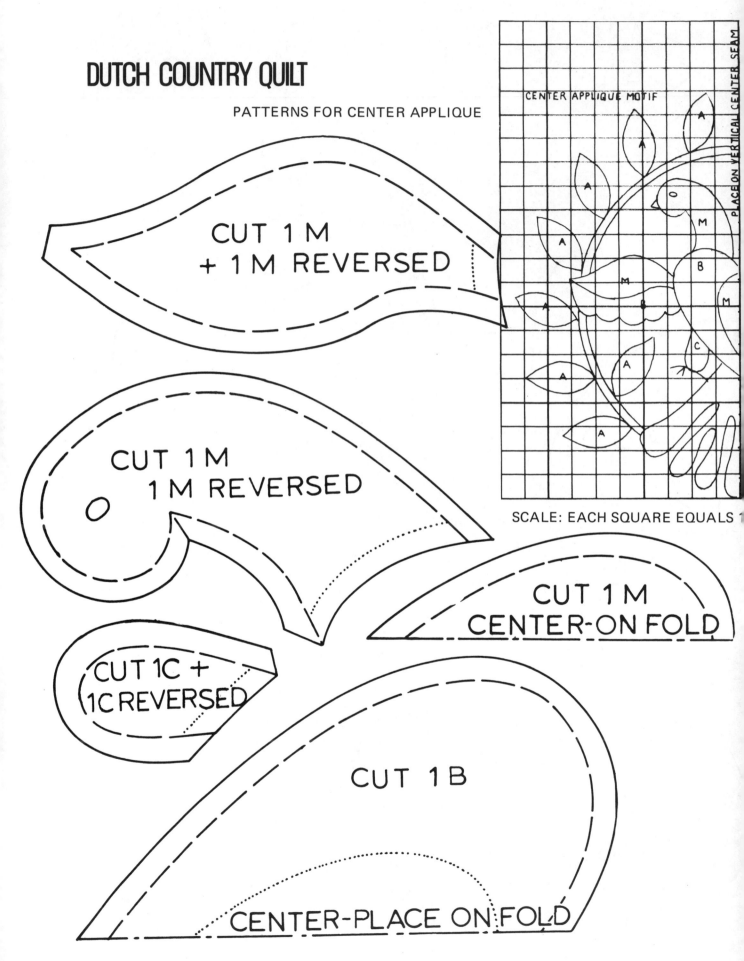

CUT 1 M
+ 1 M REVERSED

CUT 1 M
1 M REVERSED

O

CENTER APPLIQUE MOTIF

PLACE ON VERTICAL CENTER SEAM

A

A

A

O

M

B

M

A

M

A

C

A

A

SCALE: EACH SQUARE EQUALS 1

CUT 1 M
CENTER-ON FOLD

CUT 1C +
1C REVERSED

CUT 1 B

CENTER-PLACE ON FOLD

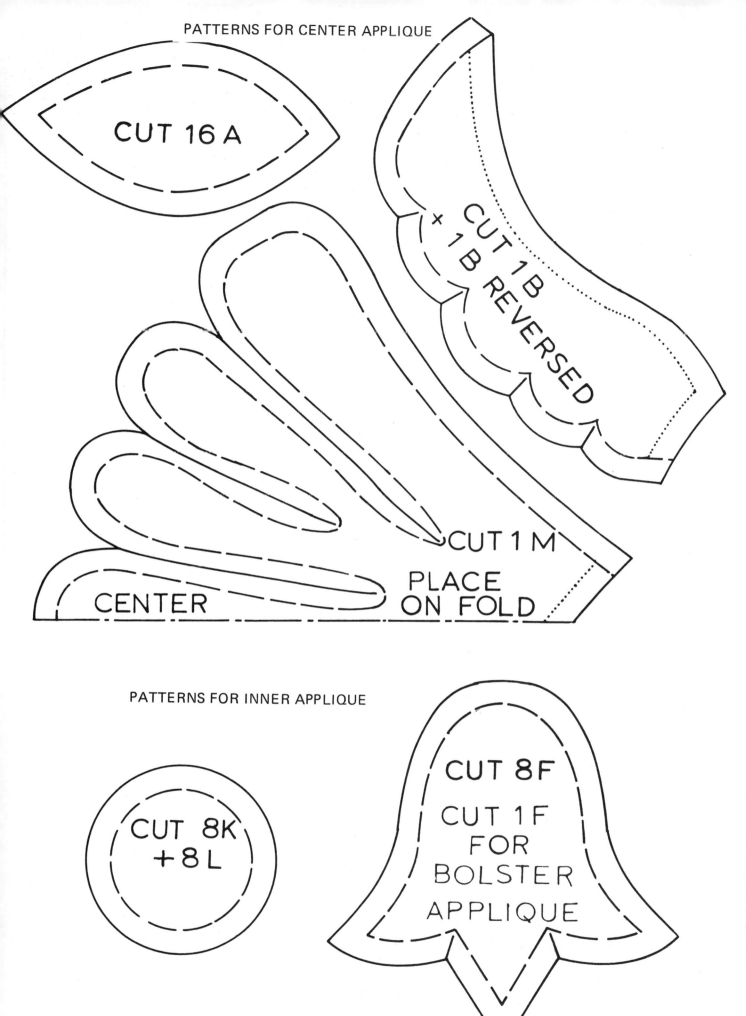

PATTERNS FOR CENTER APPLIQUE

CUT 16 A

CUT 1 B
+ 1 B REVERSED

CUT 1 M

PLACE
ON FOLD

CENTER

PATTERNS FOR INNER APPLIQUE

CUT 8 K
+ 8 L

CUT 8 F

CUT 1 F
FOR
BOLSTER
APPLIQUE

DUTCH COUNTRY QUILT

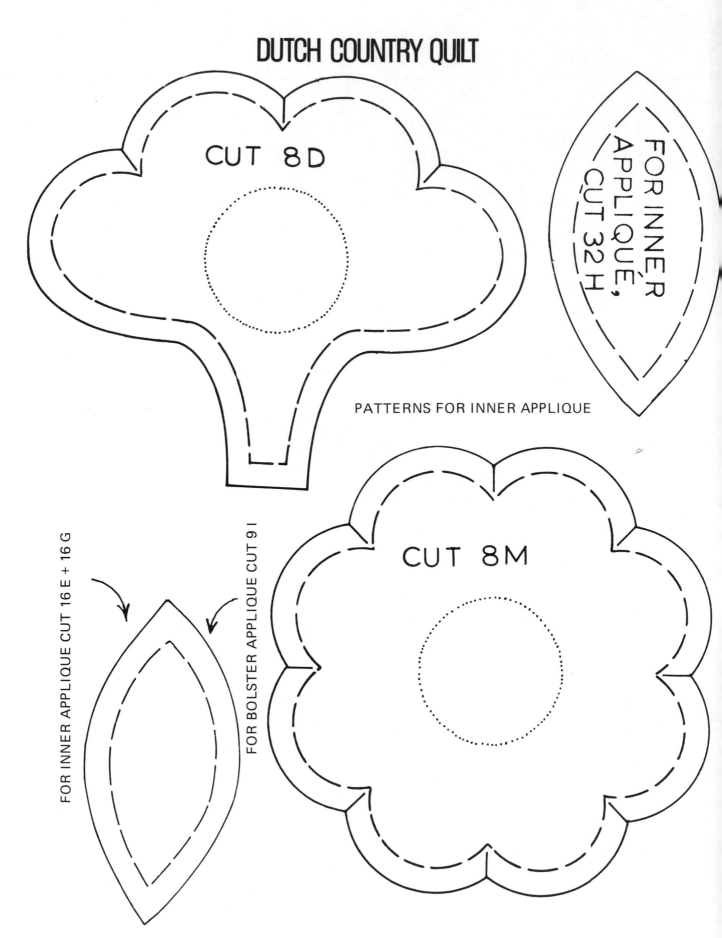

CUT 8D

CUT 8M

FOR INNER APPLIQUE, CUT 32 H

PATTERNS FOR INNER APPLIQUE

FOR INNER APPLIQUE CUT 16 E + 16 G

FOR BOLSTER APPLIQUE CUT 9 I

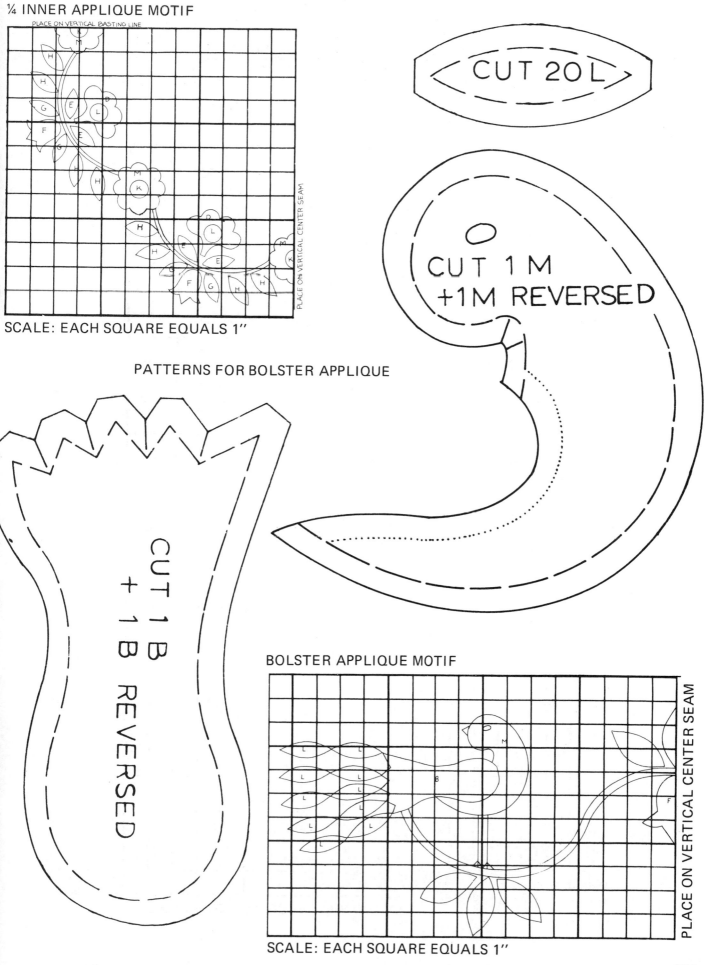

¼ INNER APPLIQUE MOTIF

PLACE ON VERTICAL BASTING LINE

PLACE ON VERTICAL CENTER SEAM

SCALE: EACH SQUARE EQUALS 1"

PATTERNS FOR BOLSTER APPLIQUE

CUT 20 L

CUT 1 M
+1M REVERSED

CUT 1 B
+ 1 B REVERSED

BOLSTER APPLIQUE MOTIF

PLACE ON VERTICAL CENTER SEAM

SCALE: EACH SQUARE EQUALS 1"

DUTCH COUNTRY QUILT

QUILTING DESIGN NO. 1
PLACE ON VERTICAL CENTER SEAM

PLACE ON HORIZONTAL BASTING LINE

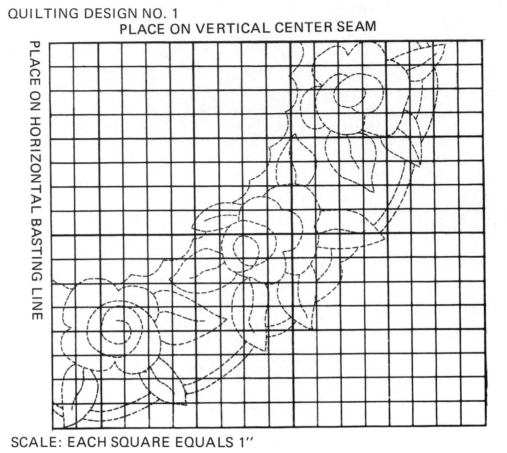

SCALE: EACH SQUARE EQUALS 1"

QUILTING DESIGN NO. 2

QUILTING DESIGN NO. 3

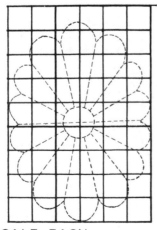

SCALE: EACH
SQUARE EQUALS 1"

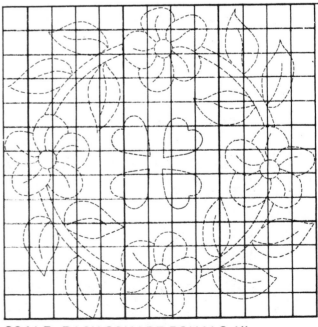

SCALE: EACH SQUARE EQUALS 1"

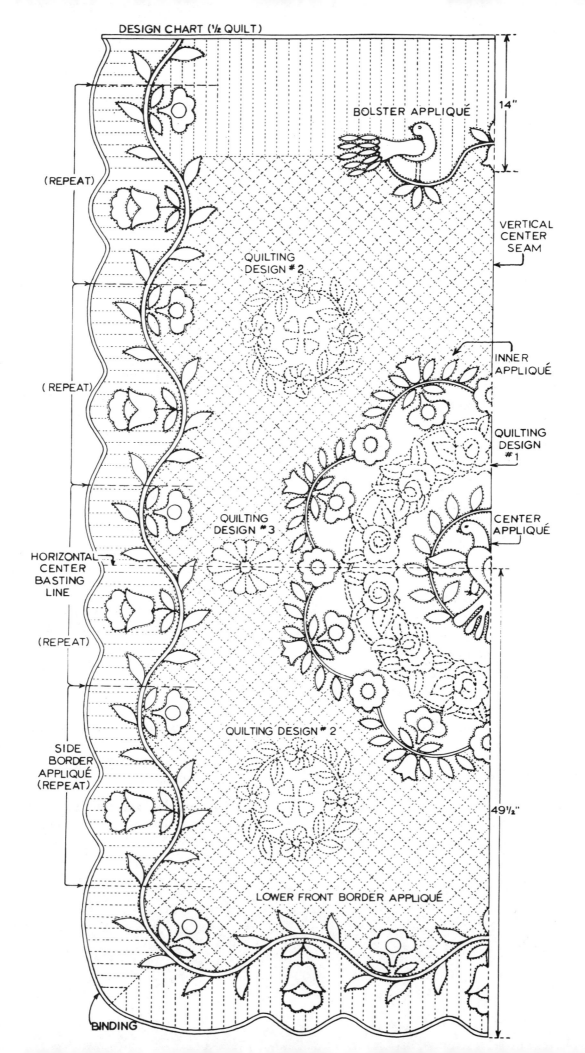

DESIGN CHART (½ QUILT)

BOLSTER APPLIQUÉ

14"

(REPEAT)

VERTICAL
CENTER
SEAM

QUILTING
DESIGN #2

INNER
APPLIQUÉ

(REPEAT)

QUILTING
DESIGN
#1

QUILTING
DESIGN #3

CENTER
APPLIQUÉ

HORIZONTAL
CENTER
BASTING
LINE

(REPEAT)

SIDE
BORDER
APPLIQUÉ
(REPEAT)

QUILTING DESIGN #2

49½"

LOWER FRONT BORDER APPLIQUÉ

BINDING

131

MEDLEY QUILT

(continued from page 71)

MATERIALS:

6 yards 36" wide blue and
white calico-type printed
cotton percale

36" wide cotton percale in
solid colors; 3¾ yards red,
2 3/8 yards green, ½ yard
yellow

7 yards 36" wide pink calico
print for backing

Matching threads

For padding, see General
Instructions

DIRECTIONS: Cutting fabric — See General Instructions. Remove selvages before cutting. ½" has been allowed for seams on center squares and borders. Blue and white calico: Cut into three lengths, each 72" long, then cut into nine 24" squares for center pieces to be appliqued. Red percale: Cut four lengthwise strips for inner border; two 4" by 70", two 4" by 76". Use remaining fabric to cut applique motifs; five "A", four "B" and 20 roses. Green percale: Cut four lengthwise strips for outer border; two 5" by 76", two 5" by 80". Use remaining fabric to cut applique leaves and stems as indicated on patterns. Yellow percale: Cut applique pieces for tulips, centers and petal inserts as indicated on patterns.

Making quilt — Run contrast basting across center of each 24" square (vertically and horizontally), to help in placing appliques. Turn under seam allowance on each applique piece (indicated by heavy lines on pattern) clipping

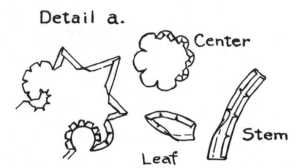

Detail a.
Center
Leaf
Stem

inner curves and corners where indicated and outer curves where necessary; press (Detail a). At center cut-outs for petal insets on Motif B, slash on long center line, clip on shorter lines. Applique motifs to squares following diagrams.

Joining appliqued squares — Pin together as shown in Diagram. Join three strips of three squares each together in horizontal seams, taking up ½" seam allowance; press seams open. Join three strips in lengthwise seams in same manner.

Making inner border — Join one 4" by 70" red percale strip to top and one to bottom of appliqued center sections, ends even, taking ½" seams. Press seams open. Join one 4" by 76" red percale strip to each side of appliqued center and ends of top and bottom inner borders in same manner.

Making outer border — Join one 5" by 76" strip of green percale to top and one to bottom inner border and 5" by 80" strips of green percale to sides of inner border in same manner as above.

Padding, backing and quilting — See General Instructions. Finish edges of quilt with narrow hem.

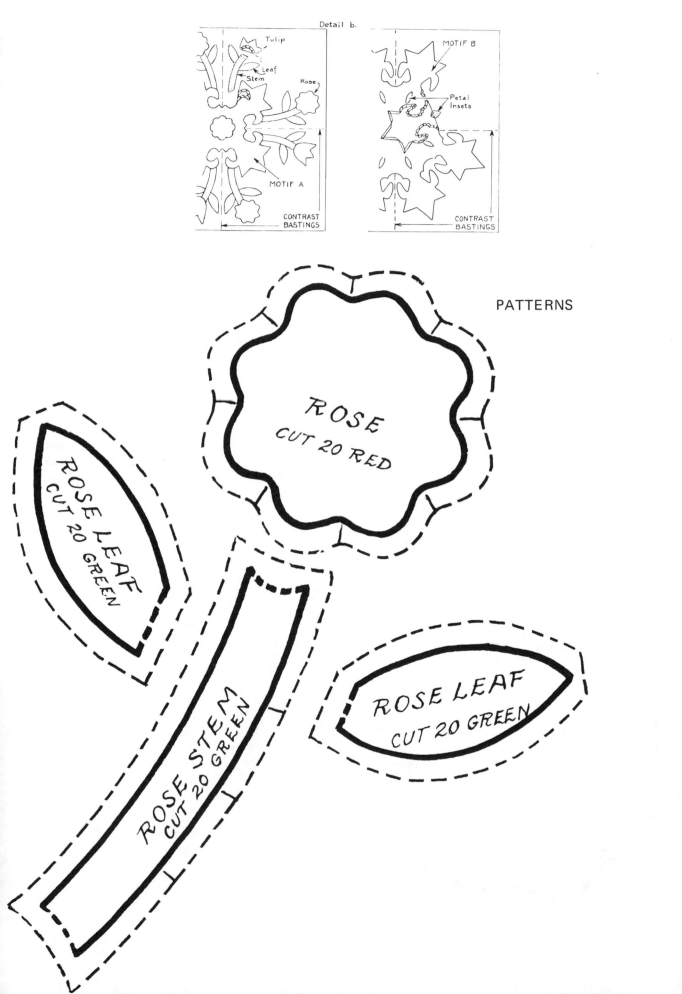

Detail b.

Tulip

Leaf

Stem

Rose

MOTIF A

CONTRAST
BASTINGS

MOTIF B

Petal
Insets

CONTRAST
BASTINGS

PATTERNS

ROSE
CUT 20 RED

ROSE LEAF
CUT 20 GREEN

ROSE LEAF
CUT 20 GREEN

ROSE STEM
CUT 20 GREEN

MEDLEY QUILT

PATTERNS

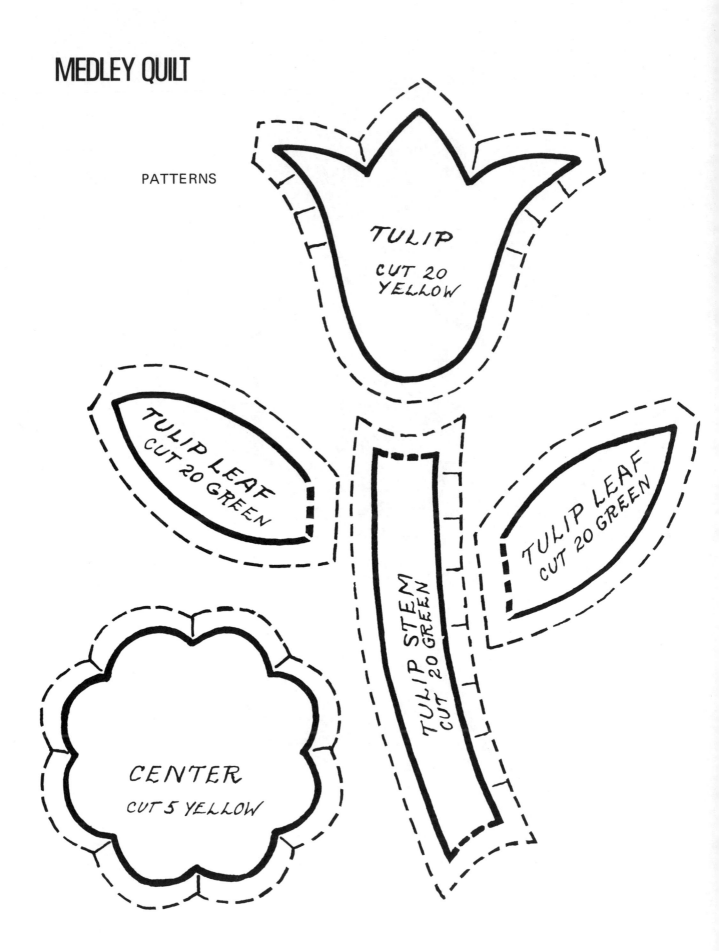

TULIP

CUT 20
YELLOW

TULIP LEAF
CUT 20 GREEN

TULIP LEAF
CUT 20 GREEN

TULIP STEM
CUT 20 GREEN

CENTER

CUT 5 YELLOW

MEDLEY QUILT

MOTIF B

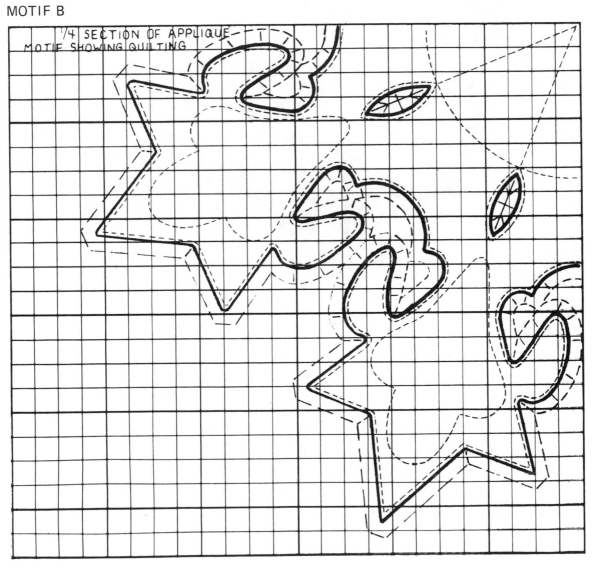

SCALE: EACH SQUARE EQUALS ½''

PETAL INSET: (AROUND CENTER OF 8-POINTED MOTIF B)
CUT 32 YELLOW

¹/4 section of quilt showing quilting on appliqué motifs – quilting on background and on border

"CLAY'S CHOICE" QUILT

(continued from page 72)

Note: Size of quilt may be changed by adding or subtracting a row of blocks. Adjust border and backing measurements and fabric requirements accordingly.

DIRECTIONS: Cutting green chintz: For quilt back, cut center panel 45" by 90¾". Next, following the cutting layout below, cut two side panels 16¾" by 90¾" (A). For outside border, cut two strips 7¾" by 90¾" (B), and two strips 7¾" by 62¾" (C). For lattice, cut five strips 2¾" by 68¾" (D), two strips 2¾" by 58¾" (E), and sixteen strips 2¾" by 12¾" (F). From remaining fabric, cut eighty 4¼" squares. Cut each square in half diagonally to form two triangles.

Cutting pink print: For inside border, cut two strips 2¾" by 76¾", and two strips 2¾" by 58¾". From remaining fabric cut forty 4¼" squares; cut to make 80 triangles. Cut eighty 3¾" squares.

Cutting rosebud print: Cut forty 4¼" squares; cut to make 80 triangles. Cut eighty 3¾" squares.

Assembly — (Use 3/8" seams.) Right sides together, stitch two triangles along the diagonal to form square; press seams to one side. Make 80 pink-and-green squares, and 80 rosebud-and-green squares.

The quilt consists of twenty 12" patched blocks set into a framework of lattice strips. To make each block, use this color key:

green   pink   rosebud

Right sides together, stitch four squares together to make strips as follows:

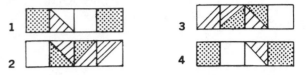

Press seams to one side. Sew strips together to form a block.

For vertical rows, stitch together five blocks with a short (2¾" by 12¾") green strip between each (A). Make four rows. Then arrange vertical rows with a long green strip (2¾" by 68¾") between each and at sides (B); stitch. Sew a 2¾" by 58¾" green strip to top and bottom (not shown).

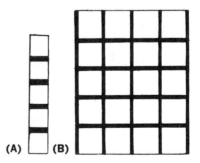

Borders — Sew short pink inside-border strips (2¾" by 58¾") to top and bottom of quilt. Sew long pink inside-border strips (2¾" by 76¾") to each side. Sew on wide green border in the same manner.

Back — Right sides together, stitch green side panels to green center panel.

Filling — Cut batting 76" by 90". See general instructions for placing quilt layers together. The quilt pictured was stitched by machine through all layers along seam lines of borders, at sides and across top.

Finishing — In place of the tufting, the quilt may be hand quilted around pieces in each block close to seam lines and along borders. Follow general instructions. Tuft all patch corners as follows: Using doubled embroidery floss (12 strands), take two small stitches in same place and tie in a square knot on the top; trim ends to 1". Remove basting.

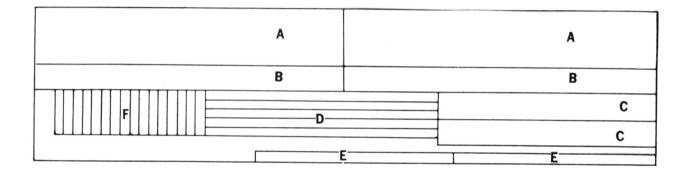

TURKEY TRACKS QUILT

(continued from page 74)

Note: Quilt may be made wider or longer by adding to width of borders, or by adding blocks at sides, top and bottom, or both.

DIRECTIONS: (See directions for enlarging patterns on page 15.) Trace outlines of pieced block units A, B, C, D and E (marked with arrows to indicate straight grain of fabric) onto medium-weight cardboard. Add ¼" seam allowance on all edges (squaring off ¼" from points), then cut out for use as permanent patterns.

Cutting fabric — Press fabric thoroughly. Remove all selvages. White fabric for quilt top: For borders, cut two strips 6½" by 84" (top and bottom) and two strips 6½" by 100" (sides) on lengthwise grain of fabric, without piecing; for plain blocks cut 49 squares, 8½" by 8½"; from remaining fabric, cut units for pieced blocks as indicated below. Red calico fabric: For outer trim cut two lengthwise strips 2" by 84" and two 2" by 100", piecing where necessary; from remaining fabric, cut units for pieced blocks as indicated below. Yellow calico fabric: Cut units for pieced blocks as indicated below. For pieced blocks, trace around each cardboard pattern for desired unit, placing arrows on straight grain of fabric. For one pieced block, cut as follows:

No. of Units	Pattern	Color
1	A	Yellow calico
4	B	
4 right side up	C	Red calico
4 reversed		
8	D	White
4	E	White

Cut enough for 50 pieced blocks. Group together pieces of a kind.

Assembly of quilt — Join units for pieced blocks according to Design Chart. Join smaller units B, C and D together first, then join to larger units. With right sides together and using fine running stitches, take exact ¼" seams; start and stop on seam lines at corners. Be careful not to stretch bias edges. Press seams open as you go. Eleven blocks form each panel (top to bottom) (see Diagram A). Join six pieced blocks alternately with five plain blocks to form one vertical panel, taking up ¼" seam allowance. Press seams open. Repeat four more times. Join six plain blocks alternately with five pieced blocks in same manner; repeat three more times. Assemble panels as shown in Diagram A so that you have alternating blocks. Join seams from top to bottom, matching horizontal seams. Press seams open.

Making border — Join 84" strips to top and bottom of assembled blocks, taking ¼" seams and extending ends evenly. Join 100" strips to sides in same manner. At corners, join ends of border strips diagonally, forming mitered seams (see Diagram A); trim away surplus fabric to ¼" from stitching and press seams open.

Backing and interlining — Cut 5¾ yard length of fabric in half crosswise. Remove selvages. Join together lengthwise, taking ¼" seam; press seam open. Trim edges so that backing and quilt top are the same size. Place quilt backing flat on floor, wrong side up; smooth it out. Place quilt batting on top, one strip next to another without overlapping, if piec-

140

ing is necessary. Lay the quilt top in place, right side up; pin all three layers together, edges even. Starting at center of quilt, with contrast thread, baste through all layers out to midpoint of all four edges; next baste from center to corners. Baste outer edges together.

Marking the quilt design — This may be done before or after putting the quilt into the frame. Simple patterns (such as the straight lines between border motifs) can be drawn directly on the quilt with pencil and ruler (see Diagram A). The border motif runs around all four sides of quilt in one direction. Trace design on fabric lightly with a pencil; six motifs on each side border; five at top and bottom. Trace design for plain blocks on each white fabric square.

Quilting — Use quilting frame or a large hoop (22" or more in diameter) to hold the fabric taut while it is being quilted. Begin at center of quilt and work outward. Thread short needle with a short length of quilting thread. Pull the knot through the batting so it will not show. Take small, even stitches, straight up and down through the layers; fasten end of each thread securely by running it between the layers. Quilt plain block designs, then a scant ¼" each side of all seams on plain and pieced blocks. Quilt border motifs and straight lines between (see Diagram A). After quilting has been completed, erase any pencil lines with art gum.

Making outer trim — Trace pattern onto medium-weight cardboard and cut out for permanent pattern. Starting at center of each 2" strip and working toward ends, place straight edge of pattern along one edge of fabric and trace shaped edge on opposite edge; trace this 5¼" repeat along entire length of each strip. Cut along market lines. Turn under ¼" seam allowance on shaped edge, clipping at inner curves, baste and press. Matching centers, pin straight edges to quilt backing, right sides together, allowing ends to extend at corners. Stitch ¼" from edges, stopping stitching at corners. Turn trim over edge, pin shaped edge to border. Turn in ends of top and bottom trim over sides (continuing design as closely as possible); trim away surplus fabric. Slip-stitch free edges of trim in place.

TURKEY TRACKS QUILT

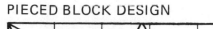

PIECED BLOCK DESIGN

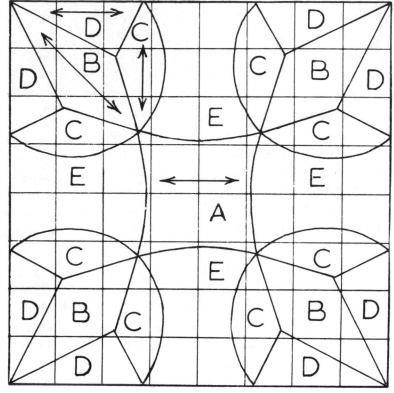

SCALE: EACH SQUARE = 1″

BLOCK QUILTING DESIGN

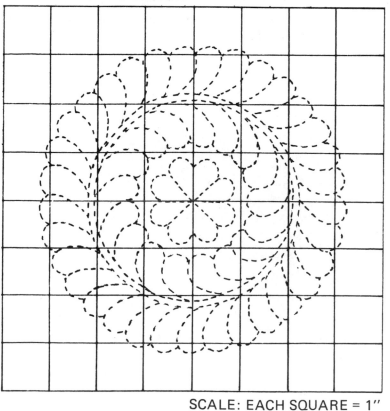

SCALE: EACH SQUARE = 1″

142

BORDER QUILTING DESIGN

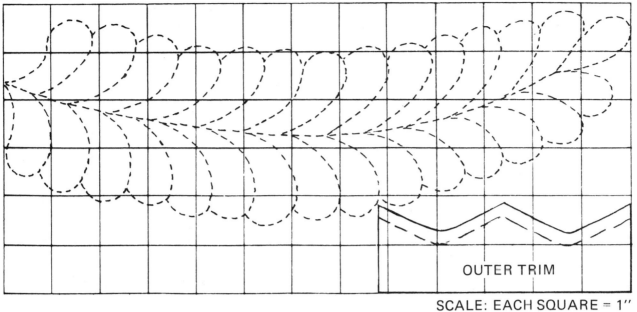

OUTER TRIM

SCALE: EACH SQUARE = 1"

"TURKEY TRACK" QUILT   DIAGRAM A (¼ QUILT)

LOG CABIN QUILT

(continued from page 76)

Note: Quilt may be made wider or longer by adding to width of borders, or by adding pieced blocks at sides, top and bottom, or both.

DIRECTIONS: To enlarge design for pieced block, see page 15. Trace outlines of units A, B, C, E, G, I, K, M, O and Q onto medium-weight cardboard. Add ¼" seam allowance on all edges, then cut out for use as permanent patterns. (Note: Units omitted above are duplicates of each preceding letter; D same as C, F same as E, etc.; mark both letters on each pattern.) Make a cardboard pattern 1 3/8" by 8" (includes ¼" seam allowance) for outer border strips.

Cutting fabric — Press fabric thoroughly. Remove all selvages. Red calico fabric: For inner border cut two strips 2½" by 70½" (top and bottom) and two strips 2½" by 94½" (sides) on lengthwise grain of fabric, without piecing. For binding, cut two strips 1½" by 88" and two strips 1½" by 108" in same manner. From same fabric, you will need 63 of unit A for center squares of pieced blocks.

For pieced blocks, trace around each cardboard pattern for desired unit onto wrong side of fabric, placing edges on straight grain of fabric. For one pieced block, cut as follows:

No. of units	Pattern	Calico print
1	A	Red (same as inner border
1 each:	D,E,H,I,L, M,P,Q	Dark background
1 each:	B,C,F,G,J, K,N,O	Light background

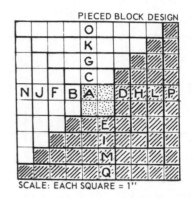

PIECED BLOCK DESIGN

SCALE: EACH SQUARE = 1"

Cut enough for 63 pieced blocks — see pieced block design for light and dark background areas. Group together same-sized pieces, separating light and dark backgrounds. For outer border, cut 210 pieces from calico scraps, using permanent pattern.

Assembly of quilt — Join units for pieced blocks in alphabetical order according to Design Chart. With right sides together, and using fine running stitches, take exact ¼" seams; start and stop at seam lines at corners. Press seams open as you go; nine blocks form each panel (top to bottom; see Diagram A). Join nine pieced blocks, turning every other block, alternating light and dark backgrounds along edge to form one vertical panel, taking up ¼" seam allowance. Press seams open. Repeat three more times (panels 3, 5 and 7). For panels 2, 4 and 6, arrange blocks as shown in Diagram A, so that when panels are assembled light and dark backgrounds are placed together, forming alternating larger triangles of light and dark pieces (see photograph). Join seams from top to bottom, matching horizontal seams. Press seams open.

Making inner border — Join 2½" by 70½" strips to top and bottom of assembled blocks, ends even, taking ¼" seams. Join 2½" by 94½" strips to sides in same manner, including ends of top and bottom inner borders.

Making outer border — Join long edges of 47 strips for each top and bottom border, 58 strips for each side border, taking up ¼" seam allowance. Pin corresponding strips to top and bottom of inner border, allowing four strips to extend at corners; stitch ¼" seams. Pin and stitch remaining strips to sides in same manner. At corners, join ends of strips diagonally, forming mitered seams (see Diagram A); trim away surplus fabric to ¼" from stitching and press seams open.

Backing and interlining — Cut 6 yard length of 45" fabric in half crosswise. Remove selvages. Join together lengthwise, taking ¼" seam; press seam open. Trim edges so that backing and quilt top are the same size. Place quilt backing flat on the floor, wrong side up; smooth it out. Place quilt batting on top, one strip next to another without overlapping, if piecing is necessary. Lay the quilt top in place, right side up; pin all three layers together, edges even. Starting at center of quilt, with contrast thread, baste through all layers out to midpoint of all four edges; next baste from center to corners. Baste outer edges together.

Quilting — Follow general instructions and Diagram B.

Binding — Join top and bottom 1½" strips to corresponding edges of quilt, right sides together, ends even, taking ¼" seams. Turn in ¼" on free edge and hem over seam on backing side. Repeat at sides, turning in ends of binding ¼".

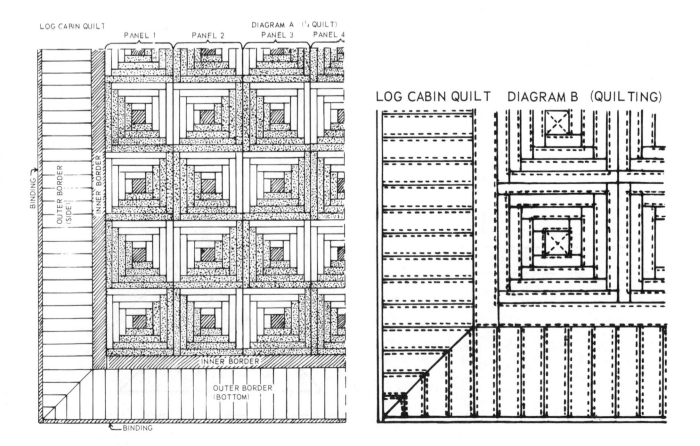

LOG CABIN QUILT — DIAGRAM A (¼ QUILT)
PANEL 1   PANEL 2   PANEL 3   PANEL 4
BINDING
OUTER BORDER (SIDE)
INNER BORDER
INNER BORDER
OUTER BORDER (BOTTOM)
BINDING

LOG CABIN QUILT   DIAGRAM B (QUILTING)

SAMPLER QUILT

(continued from page 78)

PATTERNS FOR ARKANSAS TRAVELER

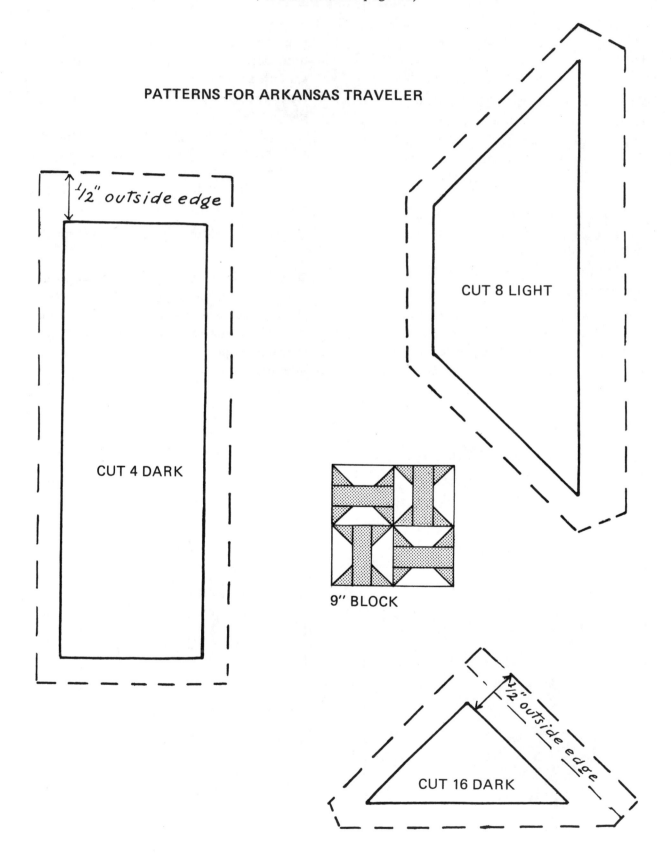

1/2" outside edge

CUT 4 DARK

CUT 8 LIGHT

9" BLOCK

1/2" outside edge

CUT 16 DARK

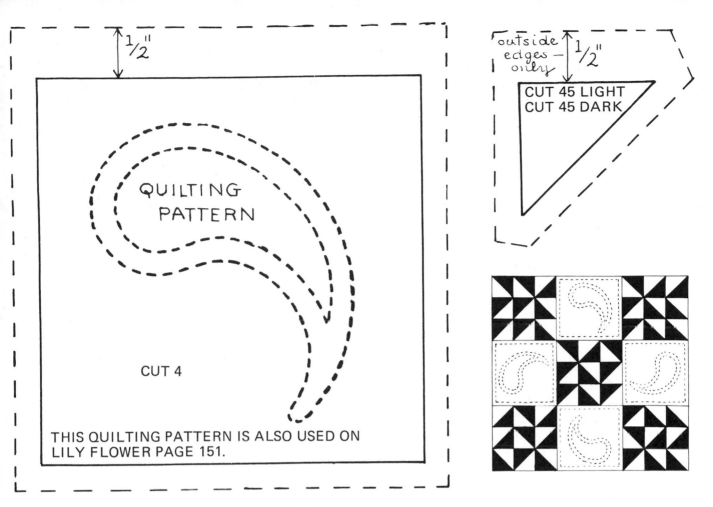

½"

QUILTING
PATTERN

CUT 4

THIS QUILTING PATTERN IS ALSO USED ON
LILY FLOWER PAGE 151.

outside
edges –
only ½"

CUT 45 LIGHT
CUT 45 DARK

PATTERNS FOR WINDMILL

PATTERNS FOR DRUNKARDS PATH

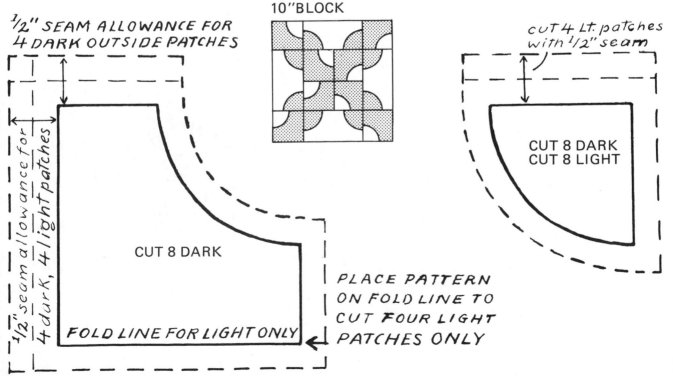

½" SEAM ALLOWANCE FOR
4 DARK OUTSIDE PATCHES

½" seam allowance for
4 dark, 4 light patches

10"BLOCK

cut 4 Lt. patches
with ½" seam

CUT 8 DARK
CUT 8 LIGHT

CUT 8 DARK

FOLD LINE FOR LIGHT ONLY

PLACE PATTERN
ON FOLD LINE TO
CUT FOUR LIGHT
PATCHES ONLY

SAMPLER QUILT

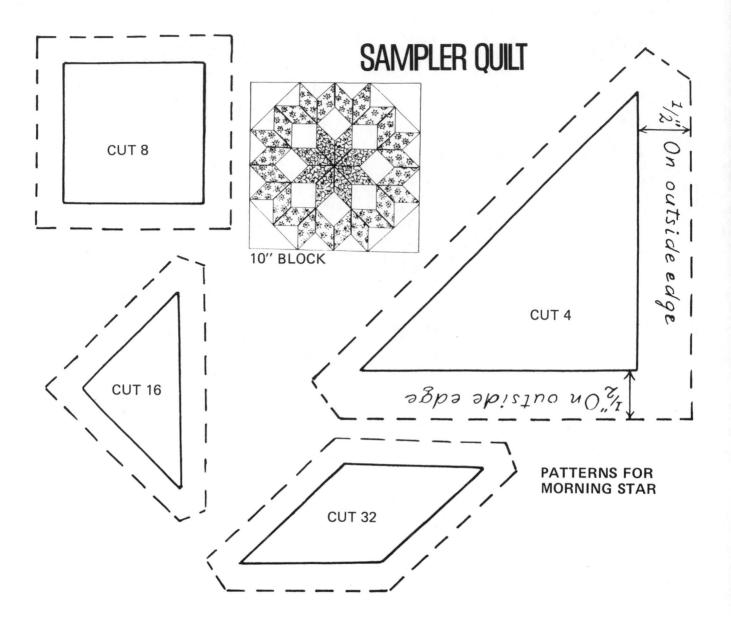

CUT 8

10" BLOCK

CUT 4

½" On outside edge

½" On outside edge

CUT 16

PATTERNS FOR
MORNING STAR

CUT 32

PATTERN FOR GRANDMOTHERS FLOWER GARDEN

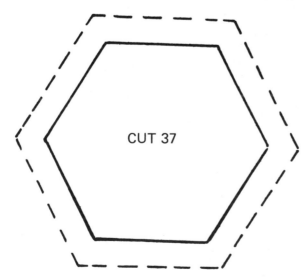

CUT 37

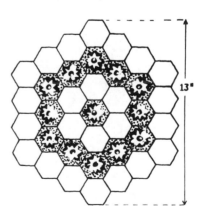

13"

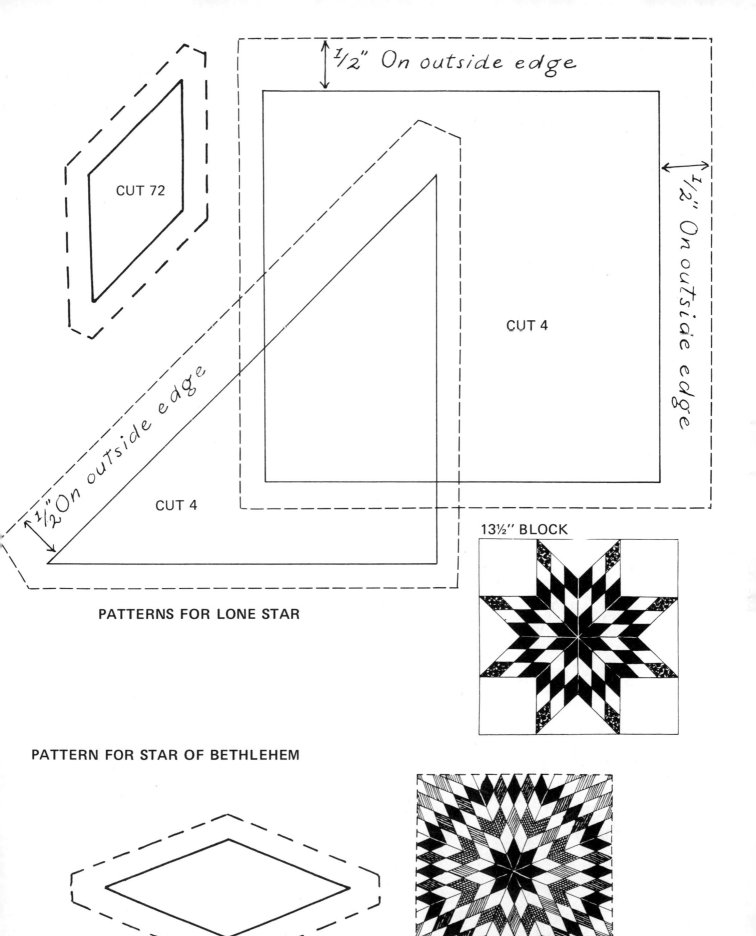

CUT 72

½" On outside edge

CUT 4

½" On outside edge

CUT 4

½" On outside edge

PATTERNS FOR LONE STAR

13½" BLOCK

PATTERN FOR STAR OF BETHLEHEM

SAMPLER QUILT

**PATTERNS FOR
GEORGETOWN CIRCLE**

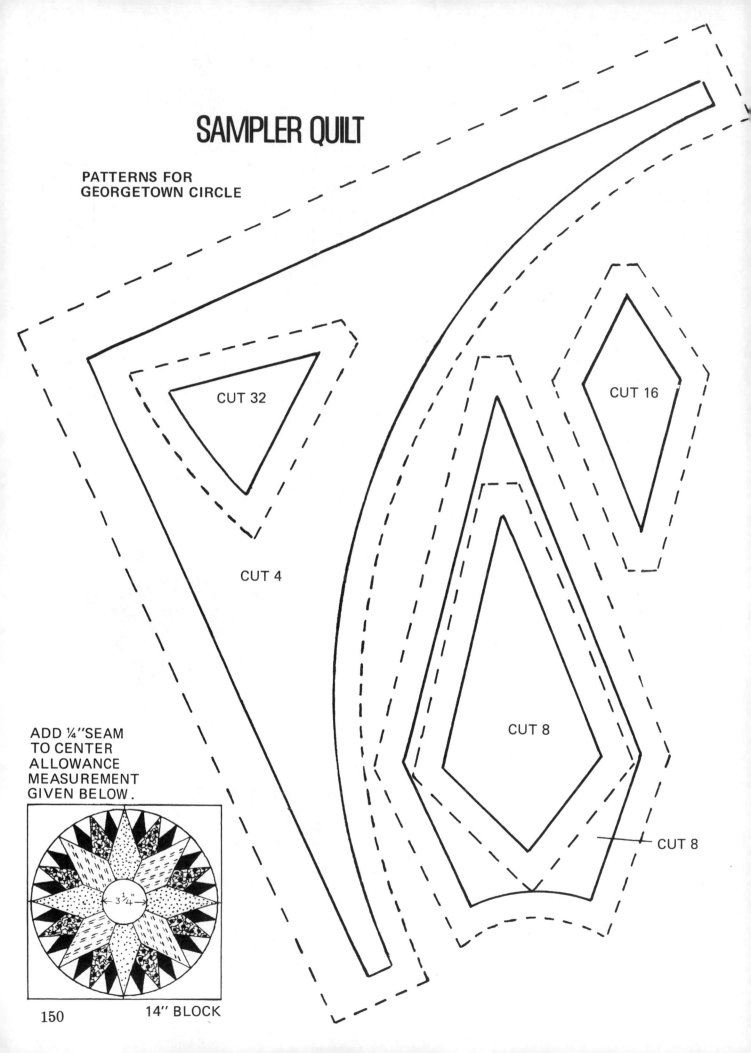

CUT 32

CUT 16

CUT 4

CUT 8

CUT 8

ADD ¼'' SEAM
TO CENTER
ALLOWANCE
MEASUREMENT
GIVEN BELOW.

3¼''

150

14'' BLOCK

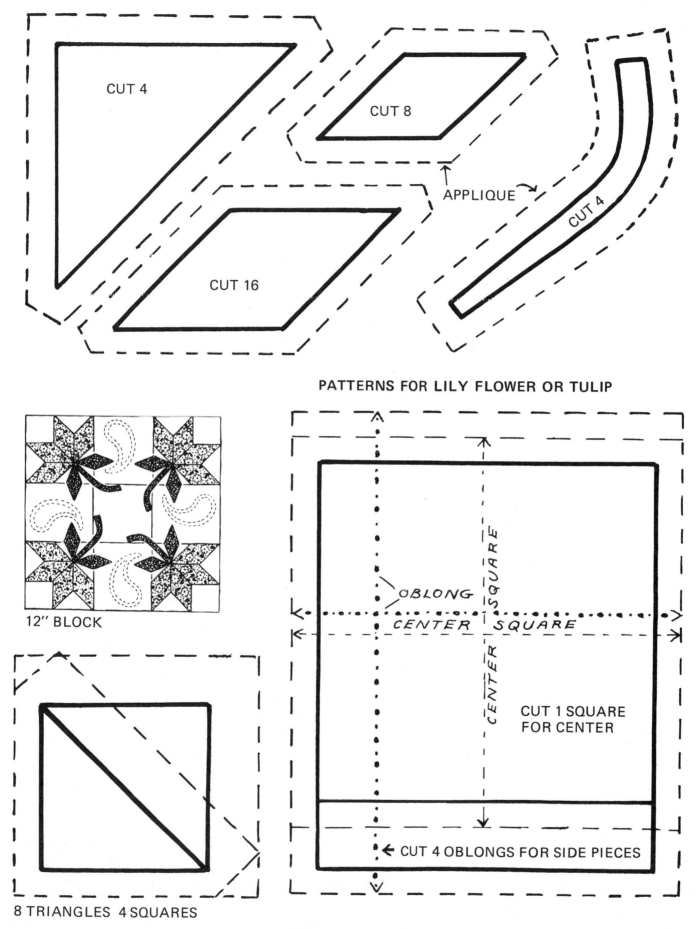

CUT 4

CUT 8

APPLIQUE

CUT 4

CUT 16

PATTERNS FOR LILY FLOWER OR TULIP

12" BLOCK

OBLONG

CENTER SQUARE

CENTER SQUARE

CUT 1 SQUARE
FOR CENTER

← CUT 4 OBLONGS FOR SIDE PIECES

8 TRIANGLES 4 SQUARES

SEE PAGE 147 FOR QUILTING PATTERN

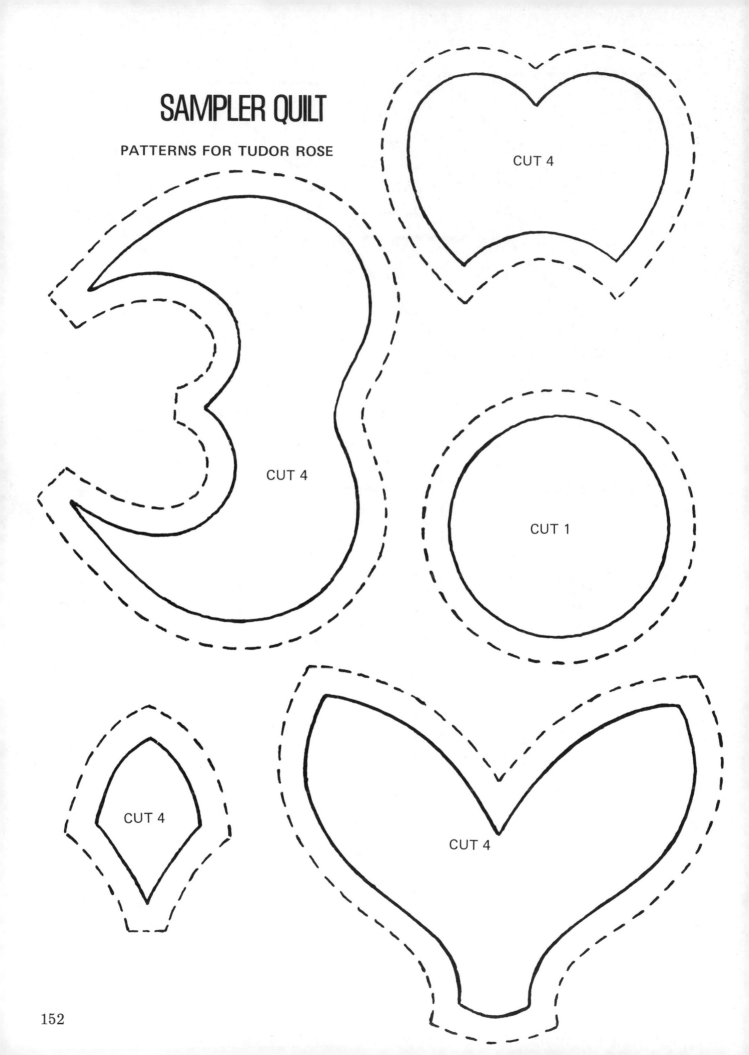

SAMPLER QUILT

PATTERNS FOR TUDOR ROSE

CUT 4

CUT 4

CUT 1

CUT 4

CUT 4

152

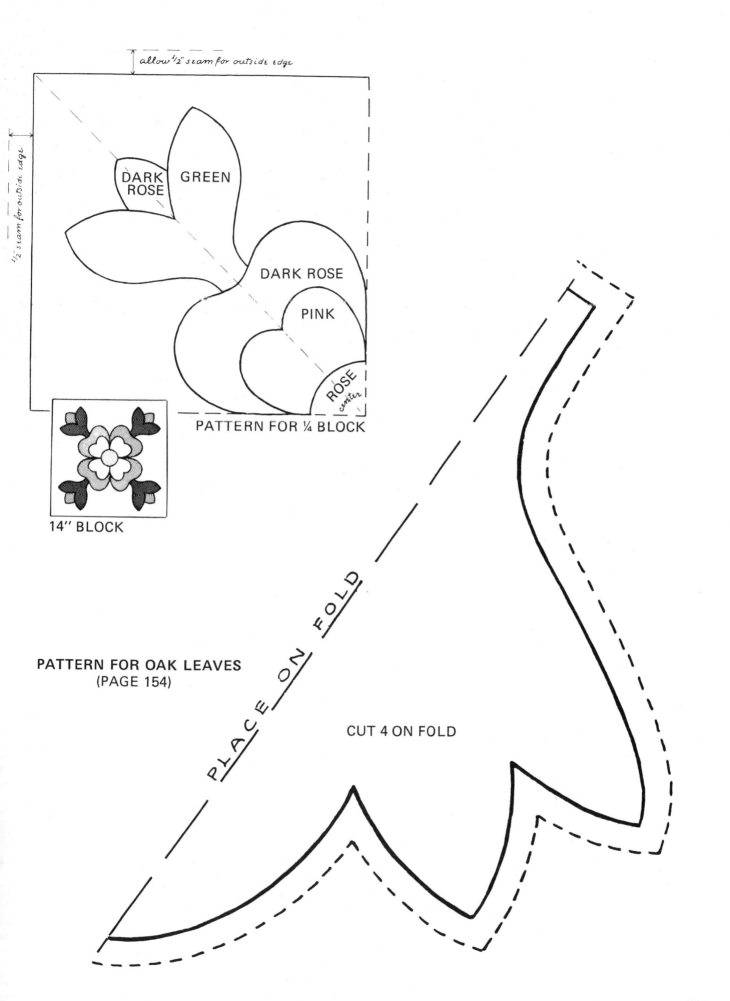

allow ½" seam for outside edge

½" seam for outside edge

DARK ROSE   GREEN

DARK ROSE

PINK

ROSE center

PATTERN FOR ¼ BLOCK

14" BLOCK

PATTERN FOR OAK LEAVES
(PAGE 154)

PLACE ON FOLD

CUT 4 ON FOLD

SAMPLER QUILT

PATTERNS FOR OAK LEAVES

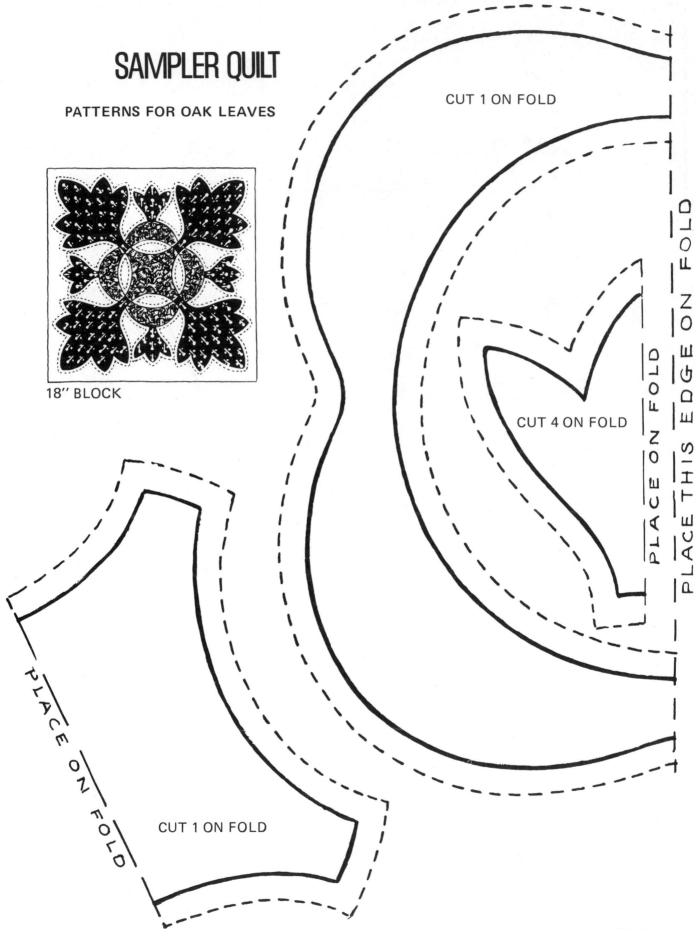

18" BLOCK

CUT 1 ON FOLD

PLACE ON FOLD

PLACE THIS EDGE ON FOLD

CUT 4 ON FOLD

PLACE ON FOLD

CUT 1 ON FOLD

SEE PAGE 153 FOR LEAF PATTERN

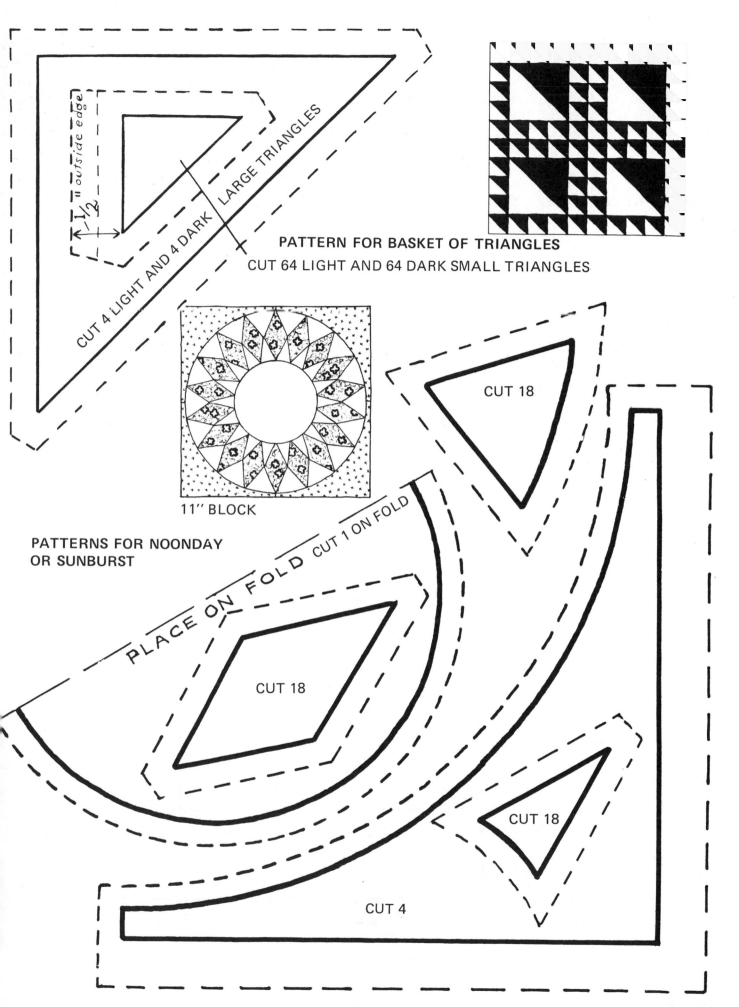

PATTERN FOR BASKET OF TRIANGLES

CUT 64 LIGHT AND 64 DARK SMALL TRIANGLES

1½" outside edge

CUT 4 LIGHT AND 4 DARK — LARGE TRIANGLES

11" BLOCK

PATTERNS FOR NOONDAY
OR SUNBURST

PLACE ON FOLD CUT 1 ON FOLD

CUT 18

CUT 18

CUT 18

CUT 4

SAMPLER QUILT

PATTERNS FOR KANSAS TROUBLES

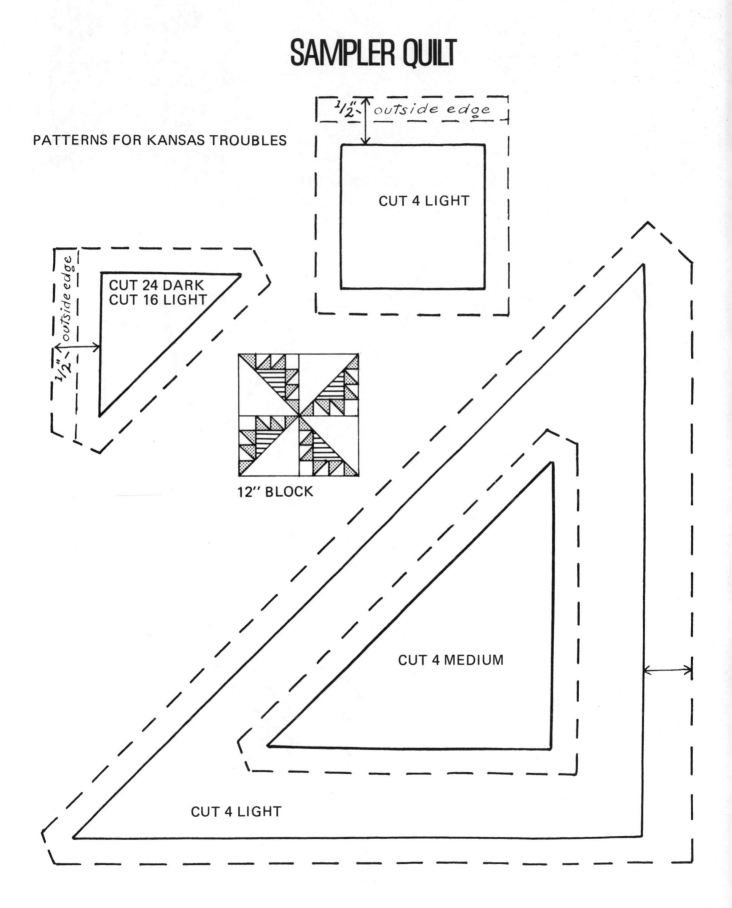

$\frac{1}{2}''$ ↕ *outside edge*

CUT 4 LIGHT

CUT 24 DARK
CUT 16 LIGHT

$\frac{1}{2}''$ ↔ *outside edge*

12'' BLOCK

CUT 4 MEDIUM

CUT 4 LIGHT

ORANGE PEEL QUILT

(continued from page 80)

Note: Quilting pattern is partially shown on diagram of quilt. Quilting should follow orange peel shapes about 1/16" outside of edge of motifs. Also quilt along center line of border all around and 1/16" from inner edge of border as shown.

MATERIALS:

6½ yards 44" wide white percale
5¼ yards 36" wide pink percale
1¼ yards 36" wide rose percale
1¼ yards 36" wide wine or
  maroon percale
4½ yards 36" wide pink print
  percale
Backing and padding (see
  General Instructions)
Matching threads

DIRECTIONS: Cutting: Appliqued center: cut two lengths of white 38½" by 103" without selvages. Motifs: trace design for "orange peel" and make several patterns of cardboard or very heavy paper. (Patterns will wear away on edges; several will be needed to keep the pieces true.) Also trace and cut several patterns of the circle given. Mark the side openings and dotted lines. Watching grain lines and being careful to place motifs close together, trace and cut the following:

> 312 pink motifs
> 88 rose motifs
> 88 wine motifs
> 352 print motifs

For border: cut two borders of pink 3½" by 103" for sides and two 3½" by 81" for ends. Cut binding from white 1½" wide and piece as necessary to fit around quilt.

Sewing — Sew the two white panels together lengthwise, taking ½" seams. Press seam open.

Marking design Measure up 4" from lower edge at center (seam line) of quilt and mark with a pin. Repeat across quilt to right and left of center at 4" intervals. Lay circle pattern on top, centering it over pin, and mark around lightly with pencil, indicating the ends of "orange peel". Remove pattern and place it on top of next pin. This will make an overlap which forms the "orange peel" design. Last circles will end about 1½" from sides of quilt. From here on rows of interlocking circles can be drawn across, one above the other and overlapping as before until quilt is covered. Last row (top of quilt) will lack the top "orange peel" in the circle.

Making applique on quilt — Using diagram as a guide to color placement, pin one motif in place. Turn under raw edges, then baste motif in place. Repeat until all motifs are basted in place. Hem motifs to background.

Finishing — Join longer pink border pieces to sides of white center panel, taking ½" seams, then join remaining border pieces to ends of center panel. Finish quilt according to General Instructions.

ORANGE PEEL QUILT

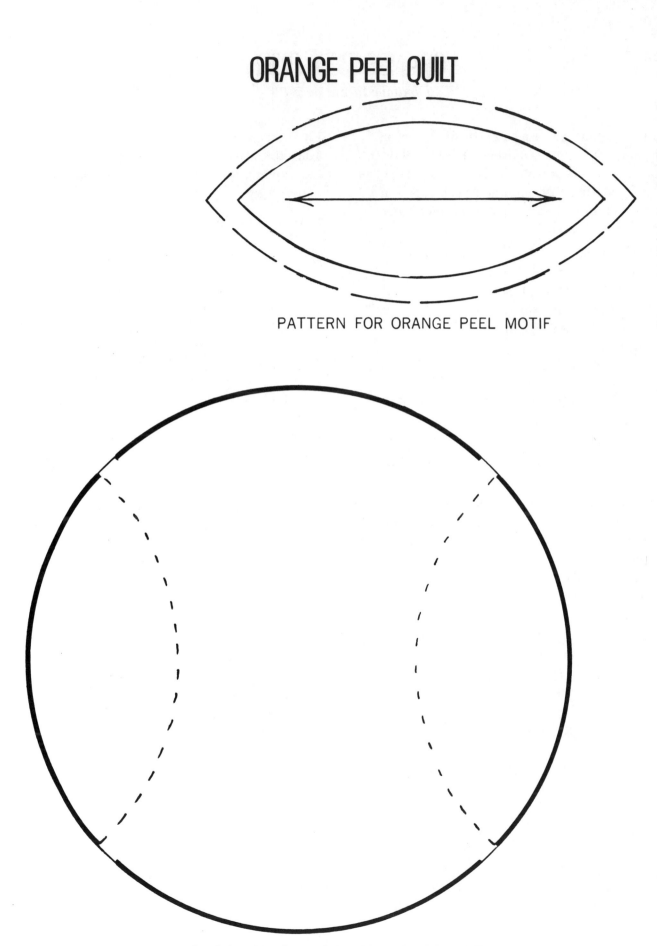

PATTERN FOR ORANGE PEEL MOTIF

CIRCLE GUIDE FOR ORANGE PEEL PLACEMENT

CENTER END

PINK – – ⬭   ROSE – – ⬭   WINE – – ⬭   PRINT – – ⬭   BORDER (PINK)

DIAGRAM OF ORANGE PEEL QUILT (QUILTING PATTERN SHOWN AT LOWER LEFT)

Editorial Coordinator: Cheryl Johnson
Assistant Coordinator: Nancy Jessup